Organizing & Storage Solutions

FOR

DUMMIES®

POCKET EDITION

by Eileen Roth with Elizabeth Miles

WILEY

John Wiley & Sons, Inc.

Organizing & Storage Solutions For Dummies, Pocket Edition

Published by
John Wiley & Sons, Inc.
111 River St.
Hoboken, NJ 07030-5774
www.wiley.com

For general information on our other products and services, please contact our Customer Care Department within the U.S. at 877-762-2974, outside the U.S. at 317-572-3993, or fax 317-572-4002.

For technical support, please visit www.wiley.com/techsupport.

Wiley also publishes its books in a variety of electronic formats. Some content that appears in print may not be available in electronic books.

ISBN: 978-0-470-59536-7

Manufactured in the United States of America

10 9 8 7 6 5

Publisher's Acknowledgments

Senior Project Editor: Georgette Beatty
Composition Services: Indianapolis Composition Services Department
Cover Photo: iStock

WILEY

Table of Contents

Introduction

● ●

*I*f you think of yourself as an organizational dummy, don't feel bad; everybody is born that way. Organization isn't inherited. Instead, organization is a learned skill set, just like driving a car. In fact that's a pretty good analogy. If you think back, learning to drive probably seemed pretty daunting at first, but driving may now be so automatic that you can practically drive in your sleep (though national safety experts don't recommend this). Organization is acquired, and as in any learning process, you need help. This book offers you that help.

I learned how to be organized through a combination of luck and sheer force of will. The lucky part is that I was born with organized parents. They showed me that everything had a place, and that some things should be put away before others came out.

After college, I landed my first job as a typist. That was fine, especially back then, before the days of career women, but I wanted more, so I decided to come up with better ways to do things to build my own rungs up the corporate ladder. I learned office organizing skills to add value to my work, and soon I'd moved from typist to secretary. The next stop was as an office administrator and eventually I ended up in association administration.

Then things really got complicated: I became a mom. Determined to spend as much time as possible with my two daughters but committed to working and staying involved, I left the office and became a Tupperware rep. Yep, parties and all. Tupperware soon had me organizing kitchens all over the city of

Chicago, coming in with my containers and leaving the place completely transformed. Being organized is a great way to win friends and influence people when you sell Tupperware. Meanwhile, I was busy with my family, washing a million loads of laundry, and racking up miles in the carpool lane. I discovered efficient ways to work and live because I had to. I couldn't be in two places at one time but my organizing systems were in place everywhere, 24/7.

As my daughters grew old enough to need me less, I reassessed, set some goals, and became a professional organizer and trainer. Today, through my company, Everything in its Place, I help clients from Fortune 500 companies as well as trade associations, entrepreneurs, and busy individuals and families get organized. What I learned in the process is that anyone can learn organizing skills and put them into practice. So if you feel like an organizational dummy now, just open up your eyes and read, open up your mind and do, and you can create an organized you.

About This Book

I'm offering you a shortcut to my lifetime of learning. In these pages, you can have all my professional secrets. Still, all the organizing secrets in the world won't do a thing for you if all you do is read them. You must put the principles into practice. This is not a novel or a book to read through and toss into one of your many piles. This book is a reference book for real life, so you have to bring the pages to life by doing.

Thinking of a task as a pie and taking just one slice at a time is a time-management trick. Do the same thing with this book, read just one chapter or a section within a chapter — depending upon your attention span and reading speed — then act on what you just read. Don't wait until you finish the whole book. That day may never come (I'm a realist), and furthermore, you're sure to forget all kinds of good tips and tricks by then. So read, and then do, and then read some more, sort of like an organizing sandwich.

First things first: Start with Chapters 1 and 2; they contain the guideposts, the principles of organization that are key to understanding the rest, and they're a pretty quick read. Next, go where you want to go. For example, if your bathroom is the war zone in your life, that chapter (Chapter 4) is your starting point.

Psychologists say it takes about 18 to 21 days to make or break a habit, so give yourself some time to absorb this information. Read a section over again. Three times if you like. No one will think less of you for it. At school, you wouldn't read something once and then take the test. (Or if you did, you know what usually happened.)

Icons Used in This Book

I direct your attention to all sorts of helpful hints for getting organized in this book with a system of icons that help you scan right to the juicy stuff on any given page. Here's an overview of what you'll see.

Cut-to-the-chase ways to clean up that mess.

Points to remember that will save you time and trouble later.

Shortcuts to shave time off tasks and leave more for living.

Extra ideas to aid the points made.

High-level hints for advanced organizing.

 This warns you of possible problems.

Where to Go from Here

You've got your Pocket Edition of *Organizing & Storage Solutions For Dummies* — now what? This pocket guide is a reference, so if you need information on organizing your kitchen, head to Chapter 3. Or if you're interesting in finding out about organizing your family and media room, go straight to Chapter 5. Or heck, start with Chapter 1 and read the chapters in order . . . you rebel. If you want even more advice on organizing and storage solutions, check out the full-size version of *Organizing For Dummies* — simply head to your local book seller or go to www.dummies.com!

I want to conclude all this talk of what's where with a reassuring word and a promise. First, there's no wrong way to use this book. Read it however you please (though if you go from right to left your comprehension may be seriously impaired). The point is simple: Read and do, and you can't go wrong.

My promise is that if you read and do just a little bit at a time, you will get results. Really. Twenty old papers tossed is an inch of free file space and the beginning of a new habit, and you can do it in five minutes or less. So get organizing today, and by tomorrow, you may start seeing things in a whole new way.

Chapter 1

Dealing with Clutter

. . . .

In This Chapter

▶ Why anyone can get organized and why you should now

▶ Stopping clutter-causers in their tracks

▶ Personalizing your organizing plan

▶ Maintaining an easy mindset to end yo-yo organizing forever

. . . .

1 know you think clutter-busting is going to hurt. For many people, getting organized sounds less appealing than a trip to the dentist and more complicated. You may have put off cleaning up your life by figuring that if you're not organized yet, you must have the wrong personality type. Getting organized goes against the grain and only causes pain.

Then there are the more specific antiorganization arguments. "I don't have time," say many, mixing up the excuse with the exact reason to do it. Others worry that organization will limit their creativity or rob them of their spark. Some people steer clear because they fear that organizing systems might turn them into uptight rule-makers or rigid control freaks.

If a broad range of people didn't share these concerns, I wouldn't have a booming business as a professional organizer. My job, in my business and in this book, is to prove the power of putting everything in its place and how that improves all aspects of your life, from work to home, play, personal relationships, and professional reputation. Why get organized? How about recovering the 15 minutes a day you spend looking for your car keys, or the hour lost last week searching for a critical computer file saved in a dark corner of your directory? Getting dinner on the table with ease and cleaning up like a breeze? Inviting guests into your home without shame?

The techniques in this book provide simple and proven ways to organize your life *the way you like to live it.* Get organized to achieve peak potential and enjoy lifelong peace.

Living in an Overstuffed World

Imagine that a tornado hit your house and whisked it away. What would you really need to start over again? What would you truly miss?

It often takes dramatic thinking to help people sort out the productive elements from the clutter in their lives. Why? Because the world is overstuffed. Houses and offices are filled to the brim, and yet advertisers still beg consumers to buy more. Sandwiches get bigger all the time, and people do too. Cities are bursting at the seams, schools are overcrowded, and they've jammed so many seats onto airplanes that passengers are practically sitting on each other's laps. Society has adopted an overstuffed mentality, and then you wonder why you can't think clearly or feel peaceful and calm.

Getting organized is about *unstuffing* your life, clearing out the deadweight in places from your closet to your calendar to your computer, and then installing systems that keep the good stuff in its place. Organizing is a liberating and enlightening experience that can enhance your effectiveness and lessen your stress every day, and it's all yours simply for saying "No" to clutter.

Clutter happens when you don't put things in place, whether on your desktop, inside the filing cabinet, in your calendar, or atop the kitchen counter. Bringing things into a room and not putting them back where they belong creates clutter. Leaving toys in the hallway, newspapers in the living room, or e-mail in your incoming queue clutters up your space. Unimportant obligations are clutter in the day. Jamming too many things in your home, office, or schedule — filling every space, littering your life — doesn't give you more power or pleasure. Random articles and activities give you clutter. By getting organized with the techniques in this book, you can leave space free to work, play, and be.

The Causes of Clutter

Clutter is costly but not inevitable — clutter is caused by patterns and practices that can be changed. If you have clutter-causing habits, I'm here to tell you that you are not alone. The age of abundance has affected everyone, and I have clients of all ages, backgrounds, and occupations who are equally unequipped to process all the information, products, and activities being pushed upon us today. You are living in a unique historical period in which people generally have more things and thoughts than ever before but are finally facing the limits to growth. You may want to simplify, streamline, get to the essence of what's important, and at the end of the day have more time and money and less stress and stuff. But how?

Let's tackle the problem at the root, by looking at the causes of clutter.

You've got mail and other forms of information overload

Whether you're hooked up to the Internet, surfing a few hundred satellite TV channels, or simply trying to get through your mail and the daily paper, you're probably faced with all the facts you can handle and more, 24 hours a day. Just a short century ago, books, newspapers, and mail were about it in terms of information arriving at your door. Today the telephone has become a fifth limb that travels everywhere you go. Radio and television bombard the population with messages around the clock. E-mail and the Internet broadcast information instantaneously, keeping millions up-to-the-minute on a world's worth of minutiae.

Knowledge is power, but information you don't need is clutter. Whether data is printed on paper, electronically encoded, or just bouncing around in your mind, information without a proper place is a waste of time and space. Getting organized will help you filter information flow and turn the tide of this new age to your advantage at work and play.

The drive to buy

Though the information age is still a little new, the consumer age is so well entrenched that buying has become second nature — whether you need it or not.

The Sunday paper beckons you out to stores. The exciting ads in the evening entertainment can leave you dissatisfied with your lifestyle and eager to make up the difference for a few (or many) dollars. A culture built on free enterprise encourages people to compare themselves to their neighbors, not on the basis of inner riches or personal fulfillment but by the number of things in their houses and yards.

My main message when it comes to managing the drive to buy is: Be very afraid. Salespeople are pros. Advertisers go to school, attend training sessions, and earn advanced degrees finding ways to sell you things without regard for your needs. Their sole purpose is to sap your bank account and fill your available space. Then, surprise! You don't end up with the more fulfilling lifestyle they promised. Your big reward is an empty savings account and an overstuffed house. Driving the drive to buy are the standard, full-price temptations. And then there are the sneaky ones.

Sale: Your favorite four-letter word

You walk into any store and what's the first sign you see? SALE!

So you make a beeline to the display behind the sign to see all the ways you can save money by buying more today. Suddenly, shopping is not a matter of looking for what you came for but of choosing from what the store has put on sale. You're no longer matching a solution to a need. The seller takes over, telling you what to buy — even if you already have a sweater in that color, or own nothing to match, so now you need to buy a pair of pants — at full price — too. As you organize yourself and your home, you'll find it easier to put up a stop sign between you and the sale sign. You'll think of your nice neat closet . . . your nice full wallet . . . and you'll just say no.

Freebies

Even more appealing than a sale to our bargain-hunting soul is that other four-letter word: free. Free lunch, free toothbrush, free trip for two to Bermuda — this single syllable is a siren call to all acquirers. But free offers usually have a price. Either the item comes attached to something else that you have to buy and might not want, or you have to buy more later, or you have to spend time filling out rebate forms and matching them to receipts and getting them in the mail.

Let's say a certain brand is giving away a free toothbrush when you buy a tube of toothpaste. Great, you think, I need a toothbrush, so you buy it. But you use a different brand of toothpaste specially formulated for sensitive teeth, and the new tube sits around forever. Was that toothbrush free? Nope. It cost the price of the toothpaste you didn't use and the space to store it.

Maybe you spend 15 minutes filling out a $1 rebate. Isn't your time worth more than $4 an hour? Add in the cost of the stamp and envelope, and you're really in the hole.

Then there are the notorious offers where you get a free book or CD if you agree to buy ten more during the year. Would you buy ten books otherwise? Do they have the books you want? At the end of the year, will you have read them all? Any? Do you have space on your shelf for ten more books?

Even true giveaways — pens, mugs, calendars, caps, knickknacks — that promote a company or product aren't free. You're advertising at the cost of the space in your life.

As you read this book and become more clutter-conscious, you'll free yourself from free things that come at a price.

Warning: This car stops at garage sales

Many cars have such a bumper sticker. The warning can at least help prevent accidents from the sudden stops, if not the clutter disaster that can result from garage-sale shopping.

I admit that I once had a garage sale problem myself. When my girls were young, they liked to take their little wallets full of pennies, nickels, and dimes and go trolling for clothes, costume jewelry to play dress-up, puzzles, games, books, toys; once we even landed a pair of roller skates. But as I started to see my house fill up, I realized what was happening: Everyone else was putting out their clutter, and I was taking it home and making it mine. How did I recover from this organizing error? I turned around and had my own garage sale. What came in the front door went out the garage door. (Now, of course, I don't let clutter in any door at all.)

Organizing principles show you that if you do buy something used, you should check to be sure you need it and that it works. Are all the parts there? Does it look nice? If it needs repair, can you take care of it easily, cheaply, within the next week?

Getting organized will also help you drive on by those garage sales and get on with your life.

The cute effect

One quick definition of the word *cute* is useless. Cute things are rarely high-value purchases, but they have a way of getting you to open your wallet. Probably the reason the thing is sending a smile across your face is because it's so silly — a wild and crazy dress you'd never wear outside the fitting room, a really dumb joke on a coffee mug, a talking tie. The problem is that cute (or stylish, or wild, or silly) wears off fast. Puppies are cute too, but you better not buy one unless you eventually want a grown-up dog.

As you discover how not to clutter up your life, you'll find yourself less attracted to things of only momentary meaning. You'll gravitate to acquiring items that will last and matter. You'll buy less "cute."

Gifts that keep on taking

A gift, almost by definition, is something you didn't choose — so you may or may not want it. But a gift is also a token of affection or esteem, so you have to keep it, right?

The important thing to remember about gifts is that they're meant to make you happy. Clutter doesn't do that. Clutter messes up your life. So observe the true spirit of giving by returning gifts you don't want to the store, exchanging them for something you can use, or putting the refund money in the kids' college fund. Maybe you know someone who really wants or needs the item. Give it to them. (Don't just pass on clutter, though. That is not the spirit of giving.)

There are occasional cases, usually involving good friends or relatives, in which the giver expects to see the gift in use. Does that mean you have to display the ugly vase from Aunt Susie or wear the so-not-you sweater from a friend all the time? Of course not. The true clutter-busting solution is to tell Aunt Susie the vase broke and your friend that the cat clawed the sweater to shreds or you spilled coffee all over it and the ugly stain won't come out — then quietly return or donate the gifts. If you prefer not to fib, put the vase away in a remote cupboard and the sweater on a high closet shelf. Get the vase out when Aunt Susie comes to visit. Wear the sweater once in a while when you see your friend. Don't let things you don't like take up prime space in your life.

Saving for later

Did your parents teach you to save for a rainy day? Great. Go have a garage sale, get rid of all the junk, and put the cash in the bank for the day you lose your job, leave your relationship, or make another major life change. Clothes you can't or don't wear anymore, old appliances and dinner plates, outdated files and papers, and extra boxes of staples simply aren't going to make the difference on that rainy day. Though *someday* may always seem just around the corner, the chapters that follow will help you make more of today by clearing away the clutter you're saving for later. Focusing on the present can yield many future benefits.

Souvenirs and mementos

Souvenirs are another form of saving for later, trying to capture a moment in a thing. When travel becomes a quest to acquire objects to remember you were there instead of devoting yourself to being there, you're cheating yourself now and cluttering up your later. Why not skip the souvenir shops and loll on the beach, lay back in a café, or take in a museum or show instead? The word *vacation* comes from *to vacate,* which is hardly what you're doing when you fill up your suitcase with tchotchkes to take back home.

Your Organizing Plan

The first step in wrapping your mind around the organizational challenge is to make a plan. How to begin? What next? Start with a basic planning tool that will pop up throughout the book. To make a plan, simply think like a journalist. No, not "man bites dog." This technique is what I call the Five W's Plus How — six questions reporters ask when writing a story, and that can put any plan into place: Who? What? When? Where? Why? How? These are easy questions, but actively answering them can help you make a concrete plan.

Organizing your mission

Why do you want to get organized? To create an organized mindset, you need a mission. Saving time, saving money, reducing stress, enhancing performance, building self-esteem, and improving relationships may figure into your organizing mission. For me it always boils down to my trademark phrase: Get organized to enjoy life.

Have you got your mission statement? Good. Write it down here.

_____

_____

_____

_____

_____

Your organizing goals

What are your organizing goals? Once you've got a mission, you can set specific objectives. Do you want to organize your home? Your office? Your time? One after the other in priority order? The point is not to try to take on everything at once, but to focus on what you want to do now. You might want to shape up your computer files or finally find the right containers for your kids' toys. Maybe the main immediate goal is to clean up your living room so you can welcome friends and family into your home. You may have one goal or ten, big ones or small ones. Perhaps your goals have a domino effect — if you get one done, then you want to do another. Can you guess what I'd like you to do with your organizing goals? That's right — write them down.

_____

_____

_____

_____

_____

_____

_____

_____

_____

Your organizing time

When's a good time to get organized? Eventually, the answer may be "all the time," but when you're just getting started, being more specific helps. Spring cleaning, fall cleanup, the new year, or start of the school year are all natural times to get organized. Knowing the family is coming for Thanksgiving can get you in gear at home. Moving? You better get organized from bottom to top.

One of the most frequent complaints I hear is, "I don't have time to get organized!" Have you ever made such an assertion yourself? The less time you have, the more you stand to benefit from organization, so break down the time barrier with five easy techniques for managing your organizing time.

Chunking your chores

Looking at the whole picture of what you need to organize can be so overwhelming that you don't get started at all. Or maybe you do, but then you quit in an hour because there's still so much left to do. Biting off more than you can chew isn't comfortable in your mouth or your mind — so chunk it instead.

When you don't have the time or concentration to complete the whole Herculean job, simply break up tasks into bite-size pieces that you can reasonably accomplish. Choose one file drawer at a time, and soon you can have the whole filing system down. Start with a single kitchen cabinet and do the second one tomorrow or next week. Rome wasn't built in a day. Chunk what you want to do and get under way.

Setting a time limit

The kitchen timer lets you know when something is done cooking. Use it to signal when you're done organizing too. When you set a time limit, things get done. You know there's a deadline, and you may even find yourself racing the clock to accomplish as much as you can before it rings. If you think you have about an hour to work, take a timer, whether your watch or a clock or the one you use while you cook, and set it for your stop time. There's a trick to this: Subtract 10 minutes from the time you want to work — for instance, an hour becomes 50 minutes — so you have time to put away what you've "decluttered."

Delegating tasks

The best way to get the job done when you're short on time is to let somebody else do it — delegate. If you live alone, delegating is called *outsourcing*. If you have a spouse and/or children, delegating is referred to as *delicate family management*. Starting out as a team often helps, working side by side to purge and organize the toy collection and home media center or clean out the garage. Eventually, as your children (and your partner) grow up, you can hand off tasks altogether, which helps them grow up further. You can find many hints for involving the family in your organizing efforts in the chapters to come, as well as for hiring out jobs when it makes sense to do so.

Being accountable

Have you ever had someone assign you an important project upon which other people's decisions, schedules, or success rode? If so, you know what being accountable is like. The repercussions of a sloppy job or missed deadline could range from wrath or a ruptured relationship to losing a job. The result is that you work hard and fast. You can put the power of accountability to work in your organizing projects simply by telling someone — a sibling, spouse, colleague, neighbor, or friend — what you've promised yourself to do. Once you've told someone else your plan, you won't want to disappoint that person or look like a failure. Being accountable spurs achievement.

Want to make your accountability really stick? There are two ways to up the ante. One is to tell someone who truly cares about the outcome. Say to your best friend or significant other, "I won't be late to meet you again because I'm finding ways to organize my time," and you may be doubly vested in planning your day.

The second way is to set a definite date and/or time for your accountability buddy to call you back and ask you if you did what you said you would. Do you know how great it feels to say, "Yes?"

Pretending to move (or really moving)

Last but not least, a powerful motivator for getting organized is to move. When you consider the cost of moving all that extra junk, and the excess stress that your lack of planning and time-management systems will cause in the process, you'll get on the stick. No immediate plans to move? Well, you could make some in the interest of the cause — or just pretend. Set a real date for the move. Schedule it on your calendar, planning backward from the move date to today about what needs to be organized by when. Put the subgoals on your calendar too, and get moving!

Organizing your space

Organization takes place in space, and a question I commonly hear is, "Where do I start?" My answer is that you have two possibilities, depending upon the situation and your personal style. They are the following:

- ✔ **Beginning with the hot spot:** Choose your organizing space by selecting the place that frustrates or bothers you the most — the hot spot. After that, everything else will be downhill.

- ✔ **Starting slow and easy:** If the hot-spot approach has you splayed out on the couch in dread and defeat, simply turn 180 degrees and start in the space that's easiest for you.

Wherever you start, you want to work where the organization is taking place. Don't pull all your clothes out of the closet and take them into the living room to sort and toss; it requires an extra step and leaves you nowhere near a mirror or a rod for rehanging. You may need to clear off some space first because empty surfaces are vital to most organizing tasks. Make like a snowplow and push it all aside.

Organizing for the people who work, live, or play here

Organization is a people-based process, designed to make people happy and productive on a daily basis — so do ask "Who?" in all the organizing you do.

To personalize your organizing systems, ask yourself, "Who works, lives, or plays here?" What do they want and need? If you've just reorganized the pantry, a few labels are worth a thousand words in terms of guiding cohabitants to finding the snack center and putting the potato chips back. Are you single or in business for yourself? Use the tips in this book to organize in ways that work best for you but remember that you may also want to set up systems that meet client needs or make a visitor comfortable.

Getting organized is one of the most personal projects you can undertake in your life. Everyone thinks, acts, and feels differently, and no single system works for every person on the planet. If there was, someone would have packaged it into a pill long ago and I wouldn't have had the pleasure of writing this book.

How You Do It

This is a trick title because, of course, the rest of this book is about how to organize. But I'm training your mind here, so take this opportunity to discover how getting organized can be as simple as 1-2-3.

1. **Pick your target:** The good news is that getting organized can improve every aspect of your life. That's the bad news too, because you can't possibly do everything at once. The first step toward using my system to organize your life is skimming the Table of Contents and choosing the target chapter you want to start with. You've already established your mission and set your goals, so this presents no problem.

2. **Read this book:** Sit back, relax, and read the chapter for your first target project. You can take notes or scribble in the margins. No matter what, you can find what you need to know and keep the text on hand as a reference all along the way.

3. **Schedule your organizing project:** Write your first organizing project in your calendar and set a deadline for completion. Break down each goal according to the sections or subsections of the chapter and set aside the time to work toward your objective. Match the length of the session to the scope of the task, whether the timeframe is 15 minutes or an hour a day, 3 hours a week, or a few work days or a weekend. Set aside the time on the schedule and go.

Maintaining Organization

Many people are hesitant to put the effort into getting organized because they doubt they can maintain an organized state of affairs. Like going on a diet, why bother if the excess pounds or clutter are just going to come back?

The beauty of getting organized is that it *does* retrain your mind, and there are no biochemical cues trying to confuse the message. In fact, organization is one of those self-reinforcing pleasures in which a mind and body, grateful for the reduced stress and strain, are eager to explore more. Enter maintenance.

If you follow the systems I describe, you may only need to have a major organizing session once a year or less to clean up any given area. A few basic tactics common to all these systems make maintenance easy. Here they are, for the benefit of your newly organizing mind:

- ✔ **Right now.** Clean up clutter as soon as you create it.

- ✔ **Every day.** Spend 15 minutes at the end of each day putting things away so tomorrow is a brand new start.

- ✔ **The one-year rule.** Every time you come across an object or piece of paper, ask yourself if you've used it in the past year. If the answer is no, chances are the item can go.

- ✔ **Plan and schedule.** If a major organizing job arises, don't sit around waiting to have the time to take on a grand action. Break it down into chunks today and write each upcoming task into your calendar.

✔ **Set routines.** Establish patterns, from the annual purging of everyone's closets before buying new school clothes and repaving the blacktop driveway to weekly grocery shopping, laundry, or housecleaning on the same day each week, and so on. Clean out the china cabinet and the garage each spring and fall. Write the car's oil changes into your calendar. Straighten up the house the day before its weekly cleaning. Purge a few files every day. The more routines that you can set, the faster and smoother things can go and the stronger your organizational systems can be.

✔ **Share.** Remember that maintenance isn't your job alone. Set up systems to share with or delegate to staff, family, and roommates.

The seeds are planted in your mind. All you need to do is fertilize them with all the information herein, and then watch your organized self blossom forth.

Chapter 2

Assembling the Tools, Supplies, and Systems

In This Chapter

▶ Using containers to put everything in place

▶ Choosing the right supplies and avoiding the wrong ones

---

*G*etting organized is a systematic process, so it makes sense that there are some systems and supplies that go into making it work. On this subject, I have good news and good news. First, the right resources can make organizing far easier than you may have thought. Second, when you assemble the right resources to get organized, you don't need many.

This chapter will introduce you to organizing resources that you'll meet more specifically in the chapters to come. *Important note:* Sit still and put your checkbook away. Don't buy a single thing or redo a space until you read the chapter for the area you're working on. That's where you can fill in the details you need to know to choose right the first time and accomplish your organizing goals. In the meantime, here's a big-picture view of how you can turn your organized mindset into action.

Putting Things in Their Place: Containers

Every time you set out to organize a space, you need containers to clean out the deadwood and create homes for the survivors. Whether you're working in the garage or getting your office into shape, the following tools and techniques can help put everything into place.

No-strain containers: Types, shapes, and sizes

Containers can organize things by like type, such as trays for cosmetics or pens and pencils or dividers for desk or underwear drawers. They can keep food fresh, as a sealed canister does your pasta or pet food. Containers can facilitate cleanup — for instance, preschoolers' toys in big open baskets children can easily access. Containers are your organizing friends.

Whenever you aim to contain, measure the item(s) and storage space first, and then search the house or hit the store for what you need. Containing options include:

- ✔ Cabinets
- ✔ Shelves
- ✔ Drawers and drawer dividers
- ✔ Bookcases and bookends
- ✔ Magazine racks
- ✔ File drawers and boxes

✔ Baskets, boxes, and a variety of closed
containers

✔ Tiered and stacking racks

Each class of container comes in a range of materials,
shapes, and sizes. Matching these characteristics to
your containing criteria is your goal — so isn't it great
that manufacturers have come out with just about
every container you could ever need?

Selecting the material

In selecting material, consider the container's weight,
durability, safety, and looks, and whether you can lift
or carry it easily. In general, plastic is lightest, lasts
long, and doesn't break. However, plastic is often not
as scenic as glass or a pretty basket. You probably
don't want plastic in your living room, but boy, is it
great in the kitchen, inside cupboards, and for storage areas.

Choosing clear or colored containers

Clear containers have a clear advantage: You can see
right through them to identify the contents inside.
Unless you're trying to hide what's in your container,
choose clear and save yourself a step. Transparent
containers are also great for showing young children
how to get organized. Seeing what's hiding inside —
crayons, blocks, toy trucks — sends an easy visual
cue for what gets put away there.

When visual neatness is your goal, go opaque with
your containers to keep their contents hidden. In this
case, you may want to use color as a code — for
instance, a blue container to hold kids' gloves and
green for adults.

Doing geometry: Shape and size

Round containers waste space. Want to picture why?
Square off a round container in your mind's eye, and
you can see the corners that you're losing. Or put several round containers together and look at all the
empty space in between. Whenever you can, choose
squares or rectangles for your containers to avoid
this geometric rip-off. Yes, you'll need some round
bowls, and a big round basket works well for balls,
but otherwise stick to the squares.

Once you have the basic geometry down, match the
shape and size of containers to what you're storing
there. Allow enough space to group things by like
type, but not so much that things get lost or jumbled
within the container or you're left with a lot of room
to spare.

Also ask yourself whether you need a lid on this container. Does it need a tight seal or stackable surface?
Some containers, such as Tupperware's Modular
Mates, stack easily on top of each other, which can
make good use of vertical space.

If you're containing food, you might consider a pour-
ing spout. Try this concept on your containers for
cereal, sugar, rice, pancake mix, and biscuit mix.

Identifying with labels

A label can save loads of time by identifying a container's contents with a quick look. Best for things
you're storing out of sight (nobody wants to sit on the
living room couch and read a label that says "Extra
Ashtrays"), container labels add information to your
organization. Here are a few tips:

✔ Be sure to use a washable label if you may be cleaning the container in question (for instance, the one you store your flour in). Skip the white computer labels and use a clear, plastic one or a tape made on a label-maker instead.

✔ Clear labels are hard to see on clear containers. If you use a clear, washable label on a clear container per the preceding point, place the label low so that the contents behind it can serve as a background.

✔ Use colored labels to code containers by type. Maybe all your baking supplies are in containers with blue labels ("b" is for blue and for baking), while pasta and grains are labeled with green ("g" for green and grains).

The Three Ds: Using containers as clutter busters

A major contributor to clutter is a basic law of physics: Matter is inert. The way to unclutter is to make matter mobile, and the Three Ds can help. What are the Three Ds? Three containers — boxes, baskets, or big sturdy bags — that you use anytime you tackle a space to distribute, donate, or dump the stuff you find there. Here's how the Three Ds can ease the flow of things and keep you clutter-free.

Distribute box

Have you ever noticed how things tend to end up where they don't belong? To bring them on home, take a container and dub it "Distribute." When you find a cereal bowl in the bedroom, don't rush downstairs to take it to the kitchen, and then go back up to collect the dirty clothes and run them down to the laundry room, followed by a stop in the front hall to grab the suntan lotion you had out for yesterday's tennis game and return it to the upstairs linen closet, and so on and so on until you're utterly exhausted. Five minutes of simple cleanup can wipe you out for the day unless you centralize operations with a distribute box.

Any time you need to leave the room to put something away, don't. Put it in the distribute box instead, and then carry it along to the next stop, just like riders on the bus waiting to exit until they reach home.

Donate box

Maybe the item is not out of place but it no longer has a place in your life. When that's the case, consider donating. Anything useable but no longer useful to you goes in the donate box, which sits there waiting to go to your sister, neighbor, or your favorite charity for a tax write-off. For instance, if you have three sizes of clothes in your closet, you obviously aren't wearing two of them, so donate those. You probably don't want to go back to the larger size, and when you reach the smaller one, you'll deserve a treat of some new clothes in today's styles. The same goes for appliances, equipment (donate or sell computer stuff the second it gets disconnected from your system; those things aren't getting any younger), dishes, furniture — you name it. Letting things move on to people who can use them makes the world a better place, and your donate box can help.

Dump box, bag, or can

 Then there are things that nobody wants or needs. You can designate a box, trash can, or big garbage bag for things you choose to dump as you unclutter. The trick is to keep it close at hand as you work and put anything you want to discard directly into the garbage. Don't forget to recycle when you can. Garage sales, consignment stores, and charities are great ways to recycle.

You can organize your giveaways by establishing a donation center in the basement or another storage area where you collect things until you have enough to warrant a pickup or a trip to a drop-off center.

A Halfway House: A container for the undecided

I am well aware that some of you have a hard time parting with things. If you didn't, you wouldn't need to hire me. Sometimes, though, all you really need is time.

Let time heal the pain of parting by putting the items you can't quite say goodbye to but know you need to into a box. Mark it with "Halfway House" and the date. If a year rolls by and you haven't gone into the box for something you wanted, then give it away, unopened. This is important. If you open the box, you're likely to pull something back out into your home. So don't. If you really want something from your Halfway House during the cooling off period, go get it. Then close up the box and proceed to give the remaining contents away if you don't pull them out within a year's span.

The Six Organizing Secrets

Every professional organizer has her or his secrets, and when I was invited to write this book, the publisher asked me to give away mine. So here they are: six surefire ways to think through organizing any space or job.

Five of the organizing secrets are acronyms, words in which each letter stands for a step of the process to make each one easy to remember. Technically, this is called a *mnemonic device,* also known as a way to help your memory. Whether you remember the technical term or not, this is a very organized way to think, and simply remembering the six organizing secrets and putting the secrets to work can help train your organizing mind.

Designing any space with a layout

When you start out to tackle a space, the ideal first question takes in the big picture: "Where do things go?" Is that the best arrangement for the desk and filing cabinets? Can you open up more space by moving the bed? What's the most efficient use of the room's wall space? To answer the big picture question, I simply ask you to think like an architect.

Even if you've never sat down at a drafting table, you can lay out any space by drawing, cutting, and playing. Specific goals and considerations for different rooms are covered in their individual chapters. For now, take a moment to review the basics of how easy it is to make like an architect and create your own blueprint for high-performance rooms. Just follow these simple steps:

1. **Draw the basic blueprint:** First, get out a tape measure and measure the dimensions of the space you want to organize, including the width of each wall, window, door, and closet, as well as the height underneath windows. Jot down each measurement as you go.

   Now swap your tape measure for a ruler and draw your room to scale on a blank piece of paper, using 1 inch to represent 1 foot. Tape two sheets of paper together if you need to. After sketching the basic outline, mark the windows, including a note about the wall clearance underneath, the closets, and the doors.

2. **Create cutouts:** Now think about what furniture and equipment you want in the room, which may include what's there now, new items as recommended in the chapters, or something that's been on your wish list. Measure these items if you already have them or estimate their dimension if not. Next, take some colored paper and cut out a rectangle, square, or circle to represent each piece, again using 1 inch to represent 1 foot as your scale. A typical desk is about 6 feet long and 3 feet wide, so that becomes a 6-x3-inch rectangular cutout.

   Continue until you cover all the furniture and equipment you'd like to include in your layout. Be sure to write what each cutout represents on the front so you don't lose track.

3. **Play with your layout:** Finally, put glue that allows you to reposition your layout on the backs of the cutouts so you can move them around on your blueprint but not lose their place, and play with your layout. Remember to use the space under windows for smaller pieces — a desk or two-drawer file cabinet in an office, or a dresser or short bookcase in the home. Also keep in mind that doors need room to open and close, so don't put the sofa in the door's path.

   Keep playing until you come up with one or more layouts you like. You may discover a whole new look for your room, or that there's not enough space for the bedroom and bureau to share a wall, all without lifting a finger or straining your back. Not bad for your first organizing secret.

Saving or tossing

From clothes bursting out of closets to the constant assault of information, most people in our affluent part of the world are buried in a daily inflow and existing excess of stuff. How do you decide what to keep and what's a waste of space and time — not to mention energy and money? Simply ask the five W-A-S-T-E questions, and you're well on your way to an informed keep-or-toss decision.

I know from my experience as a professional organizer that the process of deciding what matters in your life and what to let go of goes as deep as it gets. I developed W-A-S-T-E to help separate the wheat from the chaff. As you work through the questions, think like a judge, considering past precedent, future ramifications, and sometimes-subjective differences between right and wrong:

- ✔ **Worthwhile:** Do you truly like the dress or shirt in question? Is that article actually important to your job? If the item isn't worthwhile, toss it out now. If it is, move on to the next four questions.

- ✔ **Again:** Will you really use this thing again, or is it just going to sit in a kitchen cupboard or take up space in your files? This question could also be rephrased as, "Use it or lose it." If you don't foresee needing something in the next year or you haven't used it in the last one, clear it out. Maybe your waffle iron was used weekly for a while but hasn't been touched in months, because you broke up with the boyfriend you cooked them for or got tired of cleaning out the grooves. It was once worthwhile, but now, goodbye!

- ✔ **Somewhere else:** Ask yourself: Can I easily find this somewhere else? If you have to make waffles for a special brunch, can you borrow a maker from a neighbor? If so, you don't need to save it. Sometimes, the somewhere else is quite close at hand, such as in your own closet, cupboard, or office. Do you really need half a dozen *fix-it* outfits for painting or messy plumbing jobs when you only wear one at a time? How about the old dot matrix printer; are you actually going to send documents there with that new high-speed laser on hand? A good way to avoid this sort of redundancy is to say, "Out with the old and in with the new."

✔ **Toss:** Many things have ways of slipping and sliding by the first three questions, so here's the acid test: Will anything happen if you toss it? If not, go ahead, unless it must be legally retained.

This question often ends up taking people on a sentimental journey. Maybe something passed the first three questions because it had sentimental value, but the world wouldn't stop turning if it were tossed. This question is the toughest to judge because it can't be measured by anyone but you. The sentimental value of things generally accrues from the people who gave them to you, whether a family elder such as my Aunt Babe, a good friend or lover, or — here's a hot button — a child.

✔ **Entire:** Do you need the entire thing? The whole magazine, document, or draft? Every coordinate of the outfit, even if you only ever wear the pants? The complete catalog, when you only intend to order from one page? If not, keep what you need and toss the excess.

Breaking things down into components can help with any save-toss decision but especially when sentimental attachment is involved. Maybe you've held onto a high school newsletter that features a picture of you. Can you cut out that picture and the name of the newsletter with the date and paste it into a scrapbook, where you may actually look at it from time to time? Perhaps you inherited a painting from your grandmother that you don't like or that clashes hopelessly with your décor, but you don't want to forget. Take a photograph of it, add it to your album, and give the painting away to someone who likes it better, within or outside your family. This trick works with all sorts of things, from collections you no longer want to display to every gift you ever received that's not quite you but represents an important memory or moment. A picture says a thousand words!

Everything is the sum of its parts, but some parts count more than others. Use the entire question to trim the things you do keep down to size.

Everything in its P-L-A-C-E: Organizing space

In the course of my practice, I've developed a reliable process to clear an area of clutter, organize items for easy access and neat appearance, and fine-tune the results to your needs. P-L-A-C-E is the way to organize space and put everything in its place. What could be easier to remember?

You can clean up any area in the world with the following five steps:

✔ **Purge:** First, break out the Three Ds and the five W-A-S-T-E questions and clear your space of clutter by dumping, donating, or distributing everything you no longer need. Whether you toss the dried-up glue sticks in your desk drawer, discard outgrown toys in the playroom, or clean the hall closet of unmatched gloves and ratty old sweatshirts, purging can empower all your organizing efforts.

✔ **Like with like:** The second step in putting things into place is to organize like things together. Not only does grouping help you know where to look, whether you're searching for a file or a first aid lotion but placing similar items together also often creates what I call *centers,* one-stop spots with everything you need to complete a task. You can create a media center in Chapter 5, a cooking center in Chapter 3, and more, all to tap the clarifying effects of categorization — grouping like with like.

✔ **Access:** Once you have things grouped, place-ment is the next priority — and here, think easy access. Where do you usually use these items? Put them there. Pots and pans should be near the stove and file cabinets close to your desk. How close is close? Literally at your fingertips.

Placing items for fingertip management can enhance concentration, whether you're making coffee (hey, brewing can be hard first thing in the morning) or working on a report with multi-ple research sources. To fine-tune your access decisions, consider your fingertips first.

On the flip side, something that you don't use often can be moved farther away because you access it less. If you rarely use the warming tray, keep it on a hard-to-reach shelf.

✔ **Contain:** Containers do double duty from an organizing perspective: They keep like things together, and move things out of sight to clear the landscape and your mind. You can contain things on shelves, in drawers, with bookends or magazine holders, in hanging files, or in baskets, boxes, or closed containers in a variety of materials, shapes, and sizes. Contain within containers by adding dividers to drawers. The more you contain, the better you may feel, and you can find an abundance of practical ideas, complete with pictures and illustrations, in the coming chapters.

✔ **Evaluate:** After you complete the first four steps of P-L-A-C-E, Evaluate: Does it work? Organization is an ongoing process, and organizing can often be improved upon as your needs change or you sharpen your skills. I provide evaluation questions throughout these chapters to help you size up the success of each project as you finish it and in the future. Is a system coming up short? Adapt, change, and fix the function until you're happy that your system is doing the best possible job.

When you evaluate and adjust over time, your organization systems become self-maintaining. Some good occasions to assess your systems include job changes, starting college, getting your first apartment, getting married, getting divorced, and any time you move. But you don't have to wait for these major events to evaluate. A yearly checkup can help you keep everything working at peak level and up-to-date with your current needs.

Clearing your desktop with R-E-M-O-V-E

One very common reason people call me is that they can't see the surface of their desk and have no idea how to fix the situation short of a snowplow. That's why I developed R-E-M-O-V-E, six steps to clear off even the most snowed-under desktop and set a desk up for success:

- ✔ **Reduce distractions:** Is your desk covered with pictures, knickknacks, or this morning's mail? These may be distracting you and reducing productivity. The reduce principle helps you to identify distractions and get them off your desk.

- ✔ **Everyday use:** Only things that you use every day may stay on top of your desk. Don't worry; you'll find homes for everything else you need.

- ✔ **Move to the preferred side:** You use one hand for most daily operations, and your desk can be arranged accordingly. Placing pens, pencils, and pads where you reach for them most gives you fingertip management and makes everything from writing notes to taking phone calls faster and easier.

- ✔ **Organize together:** Just as with P-L-A-C-E, organizing like things together on the desktop forms centers so you can find and use items easily.

- ✔ **View your time:** Everybody hates to be late, so give yourself a leg up by making time visual on your desk. An organizer and a clock are important desktop elements for keeping time in view.

- ✔ **Empty the center:** Finally, chanting my mantra that "The desk is a place to do work," clear off a space in the center of the station so that you can work on the project at hand. Behold, a long-lost surface — your desk.

Responding to your mail with R-A-P-I-D

Even before e-mail came on the scene, mail overload had slowed many people down to snail's pace, so this system is designed to help you pick up speed with a R-A-P-I-D sort that doesn't even require opening an envelope. Five sort categories help you bring order to incoming mail and get it opened and filed in a flash. Here they are:

- ✔ **Read:** Anything that you need to read — later, please — goes in this stack. You may often find *to read* items at the bottom of the mail pile because they're big ol' magazines and newsletters.

- ✔ **Attend:** Notices and invitations for seminars, workshops, meetings, performances, parties, and so forth go in the *to attend* stack.

- ✔ **Pay:** If somebody wants your money, *to pay* is the pile to put the item in. Window envelopes are an easy cue. If it looks like one more credit card offer you don't want, just rip right through the envelope to protect your identity and toss, all without taking the time to open it. Time is money, and all these folks are already after yours.

- ✔ **Important:** Presume important until proven innocent, and put all unknown incoming mail into this stack.

- ✔ **Dump:** If you know at a glance that you won't read or need it, *do not* break the seal on the envelope. *Do dump* that piece of mail in the nearest available trash can.

Maximizing your time with P-L-A-N

The most important thing you can plan is your time, that precious and irreplaceable commodity. Yes, there's more to it than simply marking dates in your calendar but planning time doesn't have to be hard. All you need are four steps formulated to take you to your goals, large or small, soon or later on. Put time on your side and achieve your peak potential with the power of P-L-A-N:

> ✔ **Prepare:** The step you all too often skip in dividing up your time on Earth is defining missions and setting goals. The result can be that instead of pursuing what you want and need, you simply do whatever presents itself to you. *Prepare* repairs this problem by taking you through the "Five W's Plus How," forming the foundation for plans from next week's party to long-range career development or finding the love of your life.

> ✔ **Lists you can live by:** Out of your goals flow things to do, and the Master and To Do Lists keep track of all these tasks over the short and long term so you can do more and stress less. Once you find out how to use these lists along with your daily planner, you need never let a small detail or top priority slip again.

> ✔ **Act with rhythms and routines:** Time has rhythms, like the ticking of the clock, the beating of your heart, and the biochemical changes your body and brain go through every day. When you learn to act with your personal rhythms and establish time-saving routines, you may find more minutes in the day and reap

better results from all your efforts. From sleeping to peaking to pacing, acting with rhythms and routines helps you go with the flow.

✔ **Notice and reward your accomplishments:**
Here comes the fun part: Whenever you accomplish a goal, you earn yourself a reward, and the P-L-A-N system makes sure you get one by building a prize right into the time management process. When you notice and reward your accomplishments, you create an even stronger incentive to reach your goal the next time around. Pretty soon you have a positive feedback loop that can spiral you right to the moon.

By now, you know why you want to get organized. You have a plan for tackling organization in your mind. You've met the systems and supplies, so you can expect no confusing surprises as you work with this guidebook in the priority order of your choice. You know what you need to know. So what are you waiting for? Go!

Chapter 3

What's Cooking: Organizing the Kitchen

. . . .

In This Chapter

▷ Using fingertip management to keep cool while you cook and clean up

▷ Blueprinting your kitchen for big-picture storage

▷ Step-by-step prescriptions to cure kitchen disaster areas

▷ Handling stack attacks in your cabinets

▷ Shopping, meal planning, food storage, and recipe filing techniques

. . . .

Cooking station, dining area, phone center, study hall, and party hangout, the kitchen is often the most used and multipurpose room in the house. You're also likely to find yourself in the kitchen when you're tired, hungry, and short on patience. In such a state, causing an avalanche every time you pull a pan from the cabinet can easily send you running for take-out. The price of a disorganized kitchen can be high — but the payoff of cooling down the hot spot with organizational savvy is sweet. Clean up your kitchen systems to add flow to the heart of your home, and you may find yourself and your family better fed in mind, body, and soul.

Organizing the kitchen can seem like a big job, so don't try to tackle the task all at once. Choose a single section, such as straightening up the pantry or arranging pots and pans, to get started. Whether you work your way straight through this chapter or skip around from one section to another, your successes can inspire you to continue until everything is in its P-L-A-C-E — the word that summarizes the five steps to cleaning up your kitchen as follows:

✔ **Purge:** Toss out broken or worn items, from appliances you haven't fixed to dull kitchen knives that you don't plan to sharpen. The same goes for outgrown kids' dishes and cleaning supplies you tried but didn't like. In the pantry, fridge, and freezer, anything old or unidentifiable goes into the garbage. Say goodbye to expired coupons and untried or unsuccessful recipes. Do you have appliances, dishes, or pans that you don't use but someone else could? Donate!

✔ **Like with like:** Group items of similar type together, including dishes, utensils, pots and pans, appliances, and cleaning supplies. Arrange pantry, refrigerator, and freezer shelves like supermarket sections.

✔ **Access:** Place appliances, dishes, pots and pans, and utensils closest to their most frequent use, creating one-stop centers to make coffee, cook at the stove, serve meals, package leftovers, and wash dishes. Heavier items can go on lower shelves, while lighter things can be kept in cupboards above the countertop. Move seldom-used items to out-of-the-way cabinets or their deepest corners. Sink stuff that you don't use every day can be stored in the cabinet below.

Relocate papers, warranties, receipts, and manuals to the office/household information center (unless you have a kitchen desk) and return toys and books to their original homes.

✔ **Contain:** Move non-everyday items (appliances, cutting boards, knives) off countertops and into cabinets and drawers. Add dividers to drawers to contain their contents by type. Transfer grain products from boxes and bags to sealed plastic or glass containers. Organize recipes and restaurant reviews into binders and coupons into a 4-x-6 inch file box.

✔ **Evaluate:** Do you have enough counter space to prep foods, accommodate dirty dishes, and serve meals with ease? Can you make coffee, clean and chop vegetables and get the trimmings into the garbage or disposal, and wash dishes from start to finish — each without taking more than a step? Are you comfortable cooking, eating, and hanging out in the kitchen?

Clearing Off Your Countertops

You may have noticed that working in the kitchen can be akin to aerobic exercise, with all that bending, stretching, reaching, twisting, and the occasional hop to reach a high shelf that most of us do to prepare a simple meal. Working out while you cook may seem like a good idea in theory. However, aerobics rarely feels like a good thing first thing in the morning as you hustle to get everyone fed and out the door, or at the end of a long day when you're stumbling around bleary-eyed wondering if you can serve dinner from bed.

Surfaces you can see are a good place to start organizing your kitchen, because visible areas have both
aesthetic and practical importance. Clear counters
provide space to work and promote peace of mind
while you cook, as well as looking much nicer than
the appliance junkyard that clutters many a kitchen.

Identifying countertop criteria

Access is the key criterion to apply when clearing off
countertops. Three cardinal questions can qualify an
item, be it an appliance or a knife block, for residence
on your counter. Ask yourself:

- **Do you use it every day?** If the answer is yes,
  that's a countertop contender. Qualifying exam-
  ples may include the coffeemaker, toaster,
  microwave, can opener, and knife set. The pop-
  corn popper is probably not on this list, so put
  the machine away until popping day.

- **Do they make a convenient under-the-counter
  version?** Kitchen basics from paper towel holders to clock/radios to can openers and even
  toasters are now made to mount under counters
  and free up valuable space.

- **Can the item fit into an easy-access cabinet
  close to where you use it?** If the answer is yes,
  and this is not an everyday item, you've just
  found its new home. _Exception:_ Take into
  account the heaviness of the item and the
  height of the cupboard. You may not mind
  reaching overhead for a coffee grinder, but
  wrestling a Mixmaster out of a high or low cabinet is asking for trouble. Leave that behemoth
  on the counter unless you're only an occasional
  baker or have a cabinet that _lifts_ the equipment
  to counter height. Figure 3-1 gives you an inside
  view of this inventive technology.

Photo courtesy of Merillat Industries.

Figure 3-1: A lifting cabinet to carry heavy equipment up to countertop height.

Do you have a specialty appliance you haven't used in years but are saving for a future some-day? It could be a crock-pot, a waffle iron, a donut maker — but whatever the genius idea, someone will have improved upon the appliance by the time you want it again, so go ahead and give the space-waster away.

Arranging the countertop

After passing countertop clearance, an item needs a location. As with any prime real estate, carefully consider the space on your counter, including where an item is most commonly and conveniently accessed. The key to a cool kitchen is fingertip management, in which you arrange everything from soap to soup bowls according to a *work center* concept of accomplishing basic tasks without taking a step. Apply the fingertip management concept to everything you do to cook, serve, clean up, pack lunches, and unpack groceries. Tap the power of fingertip management in the kitchen, and even making your first cup of morning coffee can get easier. Here are some principles for easy-access counters:

- ✔ Electrical appliances need to go near an outlet the cord can reach.

- ✔ Put the toaster near the plate cupboard for easy early-morning serving.

- ✔ To create a coffee center, situate the coffee-maker somewhere near the sink so you can fill and empty the pot in the same spot. Store the coffee, filters, mugs, sugar bowl, and creamer in a cupboard overhead. For you purists who grind your own, put the grinder and beans here too.

- ✔ A can opener located near the sink makes draining off liquid and wiping up spills nice 'n' easy.

- ✔ The microwave should be in easy reach — lifting down hot dishes is a home safety hazard — and near a heatproof surface (tile counter, stovetop, or wooden board). Take into account the direction the door opens and make sure that you have adequate clearance. Microwave carts make a great solution for kitchens with limited counter space.

✔ The food processor, blender, and juicer are swing items. Store them in a cupboard if they're rarely turned on; otherwise, find a spot on the counter somewhere near the refrigerator, if possible, so ingredients are within close reach.

Clearing off your countertops can have an immediate enlightening effect that inspires the rest of your kitchen makeover. With all this wide-open space, you can shift your focus to the food you're preparing and the pleasure of the people around you. Do you feel it? Then don't stop there.

Simplifying Your Sink

The phrase "and the kitchen sink" was coined to describe anything and everything thrown together any which way. If your kitchen sink is in such a state of chaos, simplify. Stand at your sink and ask yourself: What do I do where? Answering that question can help you create your sink centers.

Creating the dishwashing center

If you have a two-sided sink, you probably wash the dishes in one side, and in the other scrape, if the sink has a garbage disposal, or rinse. Start by putting your soap, sponge, scrubber, and brush on the washing side.

Cleaning tools and supplies can get cluttered around the sink pretty quickly, so clutter-busting is definitely in order here. Soap (detergent) and sponges are the usual culprits because they're used on a regular basis. Soap may make things clean but the process can get messy. Try these ideas for spotless suds:

✔ If your sink boasts a built-in pump for dish soap, use it. This gets the bottle out of the way and provides easier, neater dispensing.

✔ As an alternative, try an attractive pump bottle for the dish soap, one purchased for the purpose or a recycled hand soap bottle in colors that match your kitchen. To prevent clogging, rinse the spout after use.

✔ Go tubular with a single soap-sponge unit, a sponge attached to a tube that you fill with soap, which means your sponge is always soaped up and ready to go. The downside is that the device can make a soapy mess while lying around, and the tube requires refilling more often than a soap bottle does.

✔ Try a nifty little sponge basket with two suction cups on the back that gloms onto the wall inside the sink and keeps two or more sponges — maybe a soft one for wiping counters and a nylon rib sponge for scrubbing pans — virtually out of sight. See Figure 3-2 for a sponge basket in action.

✔ Presoaped pot scrubbers can go into a raised soap dish with a drain to keep them out of rust-making, soap-leaching water.

✔ You can install a tilt-down panel/drawer at the front of the sink. Just the spot for your sponges.

Do you really need a vegetable brush out on top of the sink? If you're actually scrubbing vegetables every day, more power to you — but those of you who eat mostly frozen veggies or packaged salads can move this brush to a nearby drawer.

Photo courtesy of Get Organized.

Figure 3-2: An in-sink sponge holder keeps sponges handy and dry.

Under the sink: Cleaning and supply center

The term *sinkhole* may come to mind when you consider that dark place down under. Rediscover this treasure trove of usable space by setting it up as a cleaning and supply center. Placement is everything under the sink, and if yours is a tangled thicket, think access in front-to-back layers. The front layer includes anything you use every day or so — dishwasher soap, kitchen cleanser, rubber gloves (for those who are good to their hands or their manicures), and a small garbage can for things that don't go down the disposal. This is also the row for a return/repair center if you keep one here. The next layer is for less-frequently used items such as other cleansers and cleaning supplies, soap refills, and laundry detergent (if you don't have a laundry room). In the back, put your spare paper towels and sponges. Within each layer, keep like things together, using the left and right sides as natural subdivisions — for instance, the return/repair center goes on the left, cleansers on the right. Don't forget to use vertical space by stacking when you can.

Buy duplicates of cleaning supplies you also use in other parts of the house — scouring powder, spray cleanser, disinfectant, glass cleaner — and keep the extra sets close to where you use them so that you can accomplish your task without a trip to the kitchen. You may welcome the time and effort saved and be more likely to do the good deed.

To prevent unforeseen floods, keep your cleaning bucket under the kitchen sink pipes in case of leaks.

Classifying Your Cabinets and Drawers

Cabinets and drawers can attract clutter and make clatter. Nevertheless, properly classified, the secret space behind closed doors can be a cook's best friend.

Pots, pans, dishes, casseroles, and mixing bowls are usually best stored in stacks. Though retrieving an item at the bottom of a pile can be a major weight-lifting chore, so much space is saved that I recommend accepting stacks as a fact of life. Use racks with as many tiers as your shelf can accommodate to create stacks on top of stacks, making item removal and return much easier. Try the ones that expand to the height of your shelf for maximum stacking. Note that the skinny little legs of wire racks can only stand steady on a solid shelf, not on racked or grid shelving.

Two-tiered lazy Susans waste horizontal space with their circular shape, but the extra vertical tier and easy spinning access may be worthwhile if reaching is a problem for you.

Dishes: Serving centers

Decide where to put dishes depending upon where and how often you access them. The closer you keep frequently used dishes to the dishwasher and/or dish drainer, the quicker you get them put away. On the other end of the equation, you're well served to keep dishes close to where you usually use them — the stove for dinner plates, refrigerator for sandwich plates, and so on. Look for the best tradeoff between serving and stowing locations.

There are matters of altitude to consider too. Save your lower cupboards for hefty pots and pans and place dishes on shelves above the counter. Heavy dinner plates work well on the lowest shelf of an upper cabinet, with salad and sandwich plates and bowls just above.

 Make more out of a tall shelf with a three-tiered coated wire rack like you see in Figure 3-3. Putting dinner plates on one tier, salad plates on another, and bowls on the third beats making one big stack and having to move the whole mountain every time you want something from the bottom.

Photo courtesy of Stacks and Stacks.

Figure 3-3: Tiered racks expand the space of any shelf and make for stable stacks.

Glasses, cups, and mugs: Beverage center

Most people get past one sorting criteria here: If you can drink out of it, the vessel goes in the beverage cupboard. After that, it's the luck of the draw. If you ever courted disaster while reaching over a tall glass to grab a short one, you probably guessed that there is a better way.

If you have children, consider putting glasses and tall cups at a kid-friendly height so you don't have to be bothered every time a child wants a drink. Mugs can go higher up, because (unless you're raising coffee hounds) kids only use them for the occasional hot chocolate.

Make the organization of your glass cupboard crystal clear by starting with the shortest glasses on one side and working your way to the tallest on the other, in columns of the same height or glass type. No more fumbling toward the back for the glass you want. Again, if your cupboard is tall, a coated wire rack can double your usable space. Make sure the clearance between shelves accommodates your tallest glasses.

 Expanding your cupboard's capacity by hanging coffee cups and mugs from hooks in the bottom of the shelf above is best for those with good hand-eye coordination. Otherwise you risk knocking a cup off its hook as you grab your favorite mug from the back.

If there are no small kids to cater to, arranging your dishes and glasses all in a single cabinet enables you to set the table by opening only one door. Glasses are easily grabbed off the higher shelf, plates and bowls from the lower one — and dinner is served.

Pots and pans: Cooking center

Though modern metals technology has taken us a long way from the days of ten-ton cast iron skillets, pots and pans are still big and heavy. That's why you want to think *low* when you consider cabinet space for cooking vessels. Lifting up is always easier than bringing down, and don't forget to bend your knees.

You don't need access to pots and pans that get only occasional use — a big stockpot, the turkey roaster, specialty cake pans — so it's a good thing that most kitchens have so many inconveniently located spots to keep them in. Put these items in the back of deep cupboards, wedged under the support bar, in the dark and awkward corner — anywhere you wouldn't want to reach on a daily basis but don't mind once in a while.

Remembering what you've got stored in hard-to-reach cabinets can be hard. Give your brain a break by posting a list of contents on the inside of the cabinet door.

Once you divvy up the least-desirable space, put the rest of your pots and pans in the slots closest to their point of use. Skillets and saucepans can go in the bottom drawer of the stove, and baking sheets and cooling racks into a tall, narrow cabinet alongside. (If you don't have such a cabinet, get a set of dividers designed to stand baking sheets and racks on end, as you see in Figure 3-4.) Casseroles, baking dishes, mixing bowls, cutting boards, and cake and pie tins are conveniently stored under the food prep counter.

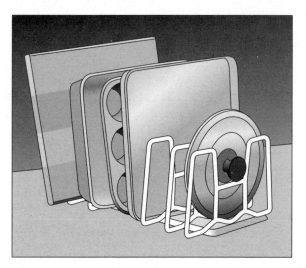

Figure 3-4: A rack keeps lids or baking pans organized from smallest to largest.

To store lids space-efficiently, put one lid knob side down inside of your stack of pans, and then layer on another lid knob side up, like a sandwich. If your lids outnumber your stack-topping slots, get a rack to stand them on end, as in Figure 3-4.

Square edges align and round ones don't, so the simple truth is that anything round wastes cabinet space. Choose square pans when you can.

Skip hanging pots on the wall where they accumulate dust and grease, and you can spare yourself the trouble of washing them before cooking. You may also appreciate the cleaner look.

Get a step stool with two steps (three if you're on the short side) to keep folded against a pantry or kitchen closet wall and put your highest cabinets within easy reach.

The Drawer Doctor Is In

Kitchen drawers can easily fall into disarray, with jumbled utensils and unsorted silverware getting in the way when you need a whisk to stir something on the stove or seek a salad fork. For drawers that do more, use the idea of work centers to create quick access to the tools for each type of task.

The essential, five kitchen drawers are:

- ✔ **Tableware center:** Placed near the kitchen table, the tableware center drawer can include forks, spoons, table knives, and serving pieces.

- ✔ **Baking and prep utensil center:** Located near the counter and cutting board, the baking and prep utensil center should include measuring cups and spoons, mixing spoons, rubber scrapers, whisks, rolling pin, beaters, hand can opener, vegetable peeler, apple corer, garlic press, zester, egg separator, grater, food processor discs, strainer, and kitchen shears.

✔ **Cooking utensil center:** Near the stove is the spot for the cooking utensil center, including spatulas, tongs, meat fork, ladle, slotted spoon, thermometers, potato masher, baster, and gravy separator.

Utensils can stay cleaner inside a drawer — but if you simply don't have room, use a utensil stand on the counter by the stove instead.

✔ **Linen center:** Designate a drawer near the stove for potholders, mitts, kitchen towels, and cloths. No linen drawer? Hang your dishtowel on the oven bar and potholders from hooks on a wall above or near the stove. Keep extras in a pantry or cabinet shelf.

✔ **Office supply center:** Freezer marker, masking and transparent tape, pens and pencils, scissors, ruler, and stapler.

If you have a few more kitchen drawers

If you're blessed with a decadence of drawers and have more to spare, here are some other ideas:

✔ **Knife center:** Chopping, slicing, paring, and steak knives can go here.

If you have small children, skip the countertop knife block and keep everything sharp put away in a drawer instead. Safety locks can keep small ones out of dangerous places such as a drawer full of knives or a cupboard with household cleaners and chemicals.

- ✔ **Wrap center:** Aluminum foil, plastic wrap, wax paper, storage bags, and twist ties.

- ✔ **Coupon, box top, and proof-of-purchase center:** Keep these items only if you redeem them regularly; otherwise, they count as clutter and should go. (Read on for hints on coping with coupons.)

- ✔ **Basic tool center:** Screwdriver, hammer, nails, and pliers. You can add tools to your office supply center if you don't have a separate drawer to dedicate. Move tools to a high cabinet if you have young children who may hurt themselves.

Divide, conquer, and contain

Once you have the right things in the right drawers, divide and conquer. Free-form drawers waste time and try your patience as you sort through in search of what you need — so measure your drawers, take stock of the size of the various items in them, and hit the store in search of dividers. Look for sections tailored to the length and width of the various things you store: standard tableware, measuring cups and spoons, gadgets, long knives, cooking utensils. Take advantage of the opportunity to give the insides of your drawers a good wipe-down before installing your new dividers. The doctor is in!

Don't buy dividers with slots molded to specific shapes, such as spoons. They limit your flexibility and drawer capacity. Get ultra-organized with the new self-adhesive section dividers that allow you to design the space to your needs.

Sectioning Off Your Pantry

The pantry has primal meaning for most of us. We worry that if old Mother Hubbard goes to the cupboard she'll find it bare — but more likely she may come across a crowded, topsy-turvy place nonconducive to putting dinner on the table or grabbing a snack.

Think of every visit to the pantry like a trip to the supermarket: You're shopping for what you need right now. Stores help you find things by arranging shelves by like type and making all items easy to access. You can do it too. To put your pantry in the pink, use these eight great pantry sections:

- **Baking:** Sugars, flour, oatmeal, cornmeal, mixes (cake, brownie, pancake, muffin), baking powder and soda, salt, extracts, oil, shortening, chips, chocolate, pie fillings

- **Cereal:** Hot and cold breakfast cereals

- **Pasta and grains:** Dried pasta, noodles, rice, rice mixes, other grains, potato mixes, bread crumbs, stuffing

- **Canned fruits and vegetables:** Fruits, vegetables, applesauce, tomatoes, tomato sauce and paste, beans

- **Canned soup, entrees, meat, and fish:** Soup, broth, pasta, chili, tuna, salmon, chicken

- **Condiments:** Mustard, ketchup, mayonnaise, salad dressings, vinegar, sauces (marinara, hot sauce, barbeque, steak, chili, cocktail, soy, Worcestershire, salsa, and so on), peanut butter, jam and jelly

✔ **Snacks:** Chips, crackers, pretzels, rice cakes, cookies, ice-cream cones

✔ **Drinks:** Coffee, tea, iced tea, hot chocolate, powdered creamers, sweeteners, drink mixes, soda, canned drinks, juice boxes, bottled water

I've seen too many pantry shelves succumb to the pressure of supersized foods and cases of soda. Avoid shelf sag or even breakage by putting your heaviest items on the floor or near support bars, and splitting up cans and jars. For instance, put fruits and vegetables on one shelf, canned soups and pastas on another, and condiments on a third.

After sectioning off the pantry, arrange items on shelves for easy access with two principles: above-below and front-to-back.

✔ **Above-below:** First group each of the eight pantry sections on vertically adjacent shelves. For instance, you may place flour and sugar on the shelf directly above boxed mixes, chocolate chips, and other baking needs. The two-shelf approach helps compact the space for each section and distribute weight more evenly.

✔ **Front-to-back:** Next, put the tallest items at the back of the shelf and the shortest in front. That means tall cake mixes line up against the back wall while pudding, gelatin, shortening, and nuts go in front. You can also use step shelves to add different levels to your front-back arrangements, as you see in Figure 3-5.

Figure 3-5: Step shelves keep jars, cans, or your spice collection from playing hide-and-seek.

Reconfiguring the Refrigerator and Freezer

Whether a science project in the vegetable drawer or a mystery package on the back of the shelf, the fridge can get scary fast. Fight the fear with some basic configuration.

Five steps to a reconfigured fridge

Like the pantry (but colder), the ideal refrigerator is arranged in supermarket-type sections with the taller items in back. You can adjust the height of most refrigerator shelves to accommodate your items without wasting space. But, you protest, I'd have to take everything out and start over! Yep. That's exactly what you need to do. (It's a great time to clean it out too.)

The following steps can take you to a cleaner, more organized refrigerator:

1. **Take it all out:** Pull up a trash bag and take everything out of the refrigerator, tossing fuzzy and old things as you go. Haven't used that mustard in a year? Goodbye! Give the whole thing a good swipe with a soapy sponge. Add an open box of baking soda to soak up refrigerator odors.

2. **Start with the obvious:** Fruits and vegetables go in the bins — fruits on one side, vegetables on the other — cheese and deli items in the drawer if you have one, butter and cream cheese in the butter compartment, and eggs in the little indentations in the door.

   If you don't go through eggs quickly, keep them in their carton instead of on the door. The carton blocks air and food odors to keep eggs fresh longer.

3. **Stock the door:** Fill the door shelves with smaller items grouped by like type — salad dressings, mustards, sauces, jams and jellies, and so on. Soda or milk up to quart size can go in taller door shelves; superspacious doors can handle liters or even gallons. The door is also a convenient spot for a carton of half-and-half or creamer for splashing into coffee.

4. **Work from the top:** The top shelf is the tallest, so this is the place for drinks. Adjust the shelf to suit your tallest pitcher or bottle. If you have split shelves, you can shorten up the other half and put your most frequently used items there (usually dairy).

Organize your bottles and cans with wire racks. Try the two-tiered type that sit on the shelf for soda cans, and a basket that hangs underneath for liter bottles lying on their sides.

The feng shui way to an enlightened kitchen

The Chinese art of *feng shui,* using placement and other techniques to improve your life force energy, is clear on its view of the kitchen: The center of the home and the place where *qi,* or essential energy, begins. Feng shui advises that you paint your kitchen walls white to cool down the heat of the stove and clear out all traces of clutter to give energy room to flow. It's nice to know that the ancient sages were organized too.

5. **Group foods by type and arrange them for easy access:** Look at what you have left to store and sort. Your sections may include cooked foods and leftovers; dairy products and eggs; meat, poultry, and seafood; and condiments. For each group, gauge the maximum height and adjust the shelf height accordingly.

Split shelf alert: A big sheet cake or lasagna waiting to hit the oven may not fit on a half-shelf. Get friendly with big foods by aligning at least one set of shelves to reach all the way across the fridge.

Freezer freedom

Now that you're cooled off, dig into the deep freeze. The same principles apply in the freezer as in the fridge: You want supermarket-like sections that make items easy to find by type. Achieve this by clearing out the contents, sorting items into sections, and selecting the freezer spots that afford best access to each group.

1. **Toss the fossils:** Anything you don't recognize or remember or can't see through the frost gets tossed.

2. **Section items off:** Good freezer sections include: Meat, poultry, seafood, prepared entrees (store-bought or leftovers), sauces and side dishes, vegetables, juice concentrates, breads, and desserts.

3. **Configure for access:** Freezer setups vary depending upon whether you have an above-fridge, below-fridge, side-by-side, or stand-alone unit. Whatever yours is, if you don't have enough shelves to make sense of your space, buy free-standing coated wire units with a few tiers. (Measure your freezer before shopping.) Next, arrange your food by section, with the items that you use most frequently closest at hand. Juice, breads, frozen vegetables, and desserts are often small enough to slip into door shelves.

"Wrap and date" is the mantra that will keep your freezer straight and your food safe. Freeze anything you won't use soon, in appropriate serving sizes. If that bargain pack of ground beef ends up wasted after thawing, you won't save money. A pound-and-a-half or so (a quarter of a 5-pound package) is the right amount to freeze for a family of four, while singles may opt to make and freeze individual patties.

 Keep a reusable ice pack or two in the freezer for keeping lunches cool or icing down an injury.

Fast-Track Food Storage

You can get more out of your groceries when you store them right. Once you set up your system, unpacking groceries and putting away leftovers becomes a snap — and the contents of your kitchen stay organized and fresh.

Don't take the word *storage* too seriously. Most meats and seafood shouldn't stay in the refrigerator more than a few days or the freezer for more than three to six months. The optimal shelf life on most unopened pantry items is six months to a year. So go do a big purge right now, and then get on a spring and fall cleaning schedule to keep your food supply fresh.

Cool container solutions

Clear is the color of choice for food containers, whether plastic bags, glass canisters, or rectangular tubs. The instant visual ID a clear container offers can save you hours, maybe even years over the course of a lifetime. Colored labels and lids can provide aesthetic relief for your eye and a coding system for your mind.

Containers that go from the freezer to the microwave serve a dual purpose and save transfer time. Remember to go square for the best use of space. Stock a variety of sizes and stack the empties inside each other. If you're storing more containers than you're using, that's a tip to toss, as are any containers without a lid or vice versa. Lid holders help contain everything in its place.

Opened packages of grain products — including flour, oatmeal, cornmeal, rice, pasta, noodles, bread crumbs, stuffing mix, and dried beans — can be protected from insect invasion by storing them in containers with tightly sealing lids. Simply match the size of the container to the contents of your package, make the transfer, and then — don't forget this part or you may be sorry later — cut out any preparation instructions from the original package, wipe them clean, and put them right into the container for reference at cooking time. Tape prep instructions on the outside if you prefer, but removing the tape and paper when it's time to wash the container can be inconvenient.

You may want to keep a few disposable containers, such as whipped cream or butter tubs, for toting food to other people's houses or sending care packages to college kids; purge the rest. Likewise, a couple of glass jars are great for storing frying oil to be reused or bacon grease until full to toss, but any more is clutter.

Some containers come preprinted with codes to match the bottoms to the lids. Use a permanent marker to code the rest with letters of the alphabet. While you're at it, write your name or initials on any pieces you take to other people's houses.

Wrapping center

A wrap and packaging center can make quick work of leftovers, lunches, and food that you want to freeze in a one-stop spot. Find a drawer or cupboard shelf that can hold all your wraps — plastic wrap, aluminum foil, wax paper, sandwich bags, resealable bags, and lunch bags — and food containers in a variety of sizes. Containers can stack inside each other according to size.

You may want to slide your wraps into one or two wire racks to keep them easily stackable. These can be a shelf-top model, or designed to mount inside a cabinet door; check out this alternative in Figure 3-6. (Be advised that large-size boxes won't fit into most racks.)

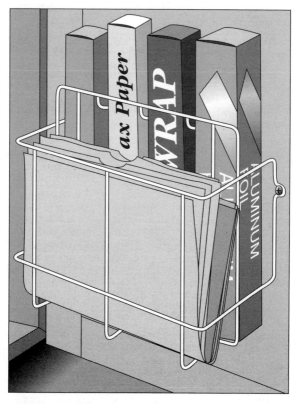

Figure 3-6: A cabinet door rack can make sense of your wraps.

If you're short on drawer or shelf space, store your wrap center under the sink.

 Resealable bags are a perfectionist's idea of nirvana. Stock all the sizes — snack, sandwich, pint, quart, and gallon — and watch yourself come up with novel ways to use them, from freezing sauces to storing children's game pieces, toting cosmetics or pencils, and making ice packs for your weekend warriors.

Once you get your wrap center set up with all of your wrapping stuff, you're ready to prepare lunches, keep leftovers, and use your freezer to maximum efficiency. Here are some pro tips:

✔ Wrap foods in freezer paper, aluminum foil, or a double layer of plastic wrap, zip them into resealable plastic freezer bags, or slip them into plastic containers.

✔ Use a permanent marker or freezer pen to label and date everything as it goes in. Just a date will do on purchased items in their original wrapping. You can skip items you go through fast and use quickly.

✔ Color-code your labels or container lids according to the section they belong to or your own criteria. For instance, I top beef gravy containers with orange lids and turkey gravy with beige. A quick-reference chart can help you decode your colors later; use the same ones all the time to remember better.

Mealtime or Hassletime: The Organized Meal Planner

Attention take-out addicts: A simple plan turns "I don't have time to cook" into "I can!" and saves time, money, and stress along the way. You may also be amazed by how much more your house feels like a home and your family like blood relatives when you fill your kitchen with enticing aromas and all sit down to break bread together. For those of you already in the nightly cooking trenches, prepare to discover some powerful secret weapons.

The first step to master meal planning is to know what you eat. Take a minute to jot down what you ate for dinner each night for the past week. (If this is straining your brain, just keep a log for the next week or two.) Now look for the pattern — maybe pasta on Monday, chicken Tuesday; meetings and school events on Wednesday mean leftovers or frozen entrees as everyone fends for themselves. Thursday is tacos or wraps, Friday dinner is out, Saturday is a slightly gourmet effort with fish or meat, Sunday night is takeout for the day of rest. Looks like you need to plan and shop for four nights. Not so hard, right (especially when you consider that most weeks run pretty much the same)?

Writing your master menu and grocery shopping list

Write up your typical week of meals, throwing in the lunches and breakfasts eaten at home. Add in any missing favorite and/or frequent meals. This is your master menu list.

Now use your menu list to create a master shopping list. Remember to account for fruits and veggies, side dishes, snacks, desserts, drinks, and school lunches. Organize your list by supermarket section, and then type it up and make a bunch of copies or enter it on your computer.

Keep your master lists on the bulletin board or in the office supply drawer in the kitchen. Use the menu list to choose tomorrow's dinner before going to bed each night (okay, it still works as you walk in the door that evening because you did your shopping in advance — haven't you?). Pull out a fresh copy of the shopping list each week and use a highlighter to indicate what you need. Add items to your current shopping list when they're halfway down. Stock a backup of anything you go through fast. Do you live in snow, earthquake, hurricane, tornado, or flood country? Keep some nonperishable items on hand for an emergency. Those who live alone can stock some soups and canned foods for days that you're sick and can't go to the store.

Add to and edit your master menu and shopping lists as you make new discoveries and favorites fall out of favor.

 Create your master menu and shopping list in a word processing table or spreadsheet on the computer so you can easily make additions or changes as your choices change.

Is making a master shopping list more than you can manage? There are two other solutions for you:

✔ Keep a wipe-off board on the refrigerator door to write down things you need as you think of them during the week. Let kids add their requests but tell them you make no promises. On shopping day, jot down the items on the board on a piece of paper. Look through your pantry and fridge and add whatever's running low as well as needs for the week's meals.

✔ Less customized but better than going listless is a magnetic shopping list with pieces to slide over the items you want to buy. Now that was easy, wasn't it?

Cooking in bulk truly saves time — and often money, because you can buy ingredients in value packs, and a well-stocked freezer or fridge can forestall many a stop at a restaurant or take-out place. Roasts, soups, stews, and casseroles are all great candidates for cooking ahead. So break out the big pots and leverage economy of scale. Remember to package the fruits of your labor in serving sizes right for one meal.

Unloading the goodies

After grocery shopping, unloading efficiently can save time and stress. Keep a collapsible crate in the trunk of the car to help carry bags into the house. Back the car into the garage for easy unloading. If you live in a high-rise building, a folding shopping cart can help you get your groceries upstairs with ease. Just remember to put the heavy items on the bottom, or they'll squish your vegetables and bread!

As you unload the groceries, be thinking about how and when each item can be used. Organizing as you unpack items can give you a headstart on busy mornings and harried meal times. For instance, wash and ice the minicarrots for the kids to snack on. Seal pretzels into resealable plastic bags to tuck into lunches. Toss out all those old and spoiled things you come across as you put away the new.

Are you a victim of grocery bag buildup? Here's how to keep bags neat until you recycle or reuse: Open one brown grocery bag, close the rest, and slip them lengthwise into the open

bag. Plastic grocery bags can be packed inside
one open bag too, or purchase a cylindrical container that hangs from the wall to hold them.
Unless you go to the grocery only once a year,
you shouldn't need more than a bagful of empty
bags on hand for reuse, so recycle the rest.

Cookbooks and Recipes

The recipes that tell us what to do for delicious success
can be a source of vital sustenance and heritage —
when they're not cluttering the kitchen with information
overload. Systematize your cookbooks and recipes into
accessible references instead of acres of meaningless
paper, and watch your culinary prowess soar.

Cleaning up your cookbook collection

How many cookbooks is enough? Everybody needs at
least one all-purpose cookbook, so that whether you
wonder what to do with the fresh Muscovy duck you
just bought or are summoned to provide oatmeal
cookies for the school bake sale, you have somewhere to turn. Beyond that, it's a question of how
much you (really, actually) cook. Go through your
cookbook collection and purge anything you haven't
consulted or cooked from in a year, even if the book
was a gift or a quaint collection from your local junior
league. Remember that the library is well stocked
with cookbooks for that special occasion when you
need an appetizer from Afghanistan. Resist the urge
to buy new cookbooks you don't need. Store cookbooks in the kitchen, where they're used. You can
contain them on a pantry shelf, install a shelf on the
wall, or, if your collection is legitimately large,
arrange them in a small freestanding bookshelf,
grouped by type. If you're stuck with a wire rack

shelf, lay a board or sheet of clear, hard plastic over it so you can slide books in and out easily. Don't forget bookends to keep everything standing up straight.

 While you cook, slip your cookbook into a clear stand that holds it upright and keeps the book open for easy viewing while screening out the splashes and spatters.

Reducing your recipe burden

Now, as for all those recipe clippings, that ragged and yellowing pile — yes, you know you have one, so put your guilt aside. Notice how they just sort of fall out all over the place when you have to find a recipe? This calls for some action. Your step-by-step solution is as follows:

1. **Get two three-ring binders and a stack of plastic sheet protectors.**

2. **Sort your recipes into two piles: *to try* and *tried and true*.** Toss out anything you tried and haven't loved, lost interest in, recipes dated over a year back or those so old the paper the concoction is printed on turned yellow.

3. **Write today's date on the recipes in the *to try* pile.**

4. **Slip recipes into sheet protectors, fitting in as many as you can see.** File the recipes, one pile per binder, according to sections marked with tabbed dividers — appetizers, meats, poultry, seafood, pasta, desserts, and so forth. Label the binder spines so you can distinguish the tried from the new.

Card files are a hard-work way to store recipes. You have to do amazing feats of origami to get the recipes clipped in a way that they fit on the card, or rewrite the whole thing from scratch. Try the binder approach and spare yourself the extra effort. To maintain your binders, throw away any recipe you try but don't like, and move those you do into the *tried and true* binder. Date all new *to try* recipes as you file them, and toss them after they've sat around for a year. Chances are that the dishes don't really fit your lifestyle, and there are plenty of new ones coming.

If you collect restaurant reviews, use the same two-binder system to file them and guide your decision when it's time to go out. Make sections like restaurant guidebooks — business lunch, romantic dinner, family, ethnic cuisines, and the like.

 If you're a serious cook and computer-savvy, you may want to consider filing your recipes on your computer, in special recipe software that also runs nutritional analyses and generates shopping lists, or in your word processing program. Recipe programs are set up to organize your recipes by section; if you use a word processor, create a different folder for each type of dish. Getting recipes entered takes extra time, but you save storage space and can print a fresh copy whenever you need one.

Coupons: Turn Clutter into Cash in Hand

Coupons appeal to our most basic instinct: to get a good deal. Of course, manufacturers wouldn't offer them if coupons weren't a good deal for them too, and purveyors love nothing more than consumers buying stuff they don't need or wouldn't buy otherwise — preferably in the extra-large size stipulated on the coupon — simply to *save* 50 cents. The first rule for turning coupons into cash in hand is *don't clip* anything you don't need. Because bagel bites are on sale is no reason to introduce bagel bites to your diet; a single person doesn't need a 2-pound pack of lunch meat; and yes, you can have too many cans of tomatoes.

However, when coupons are properly clipped, filed, and redeemed, they can be great money-savers, especially for larger families. The trick is to be efficient enough that you don't spend more time than the money you save is worth. Here's the plan:

1. **Get a 4-x-6-inch file box (3-x-5 inches is too small for wider coupons).**

2. **Add tabbed dividers and label them by five categories: food, household items, paper goods, personal, and other (batteries, camera, office and school supplies).** Depending upon your shopping habits, subdivide further for easy retrieval.

3. **Tackle your coupons as soon as they arrive — the Sunday paper is a good source — and clip items you commonly use, know you need, or genuinely want to try.** Don't bother with things that you already stocked up on unless the expiration date is fairly distant.

4. **File your coupons by section, putting the newest ones in back and weeding out those that have expired.**

For fast-food and take-out coupons, contain them in a big (6-x-5-inch) magnetic pocket posted on the less-visible side of the refrigerator. Keep menus in front and coupons in back, organized by type of food: burgers, pizza, chicken, Chinese, and so on. Purge expired coupons every month or two.

When you shop, look for a place that redeems coupons at double their face value — usually large supermarkets, where you can do much of your drugstore shopping these days too. Mark the coupons that you know you want to use on your shopping list, and then take the whole box along for the ride so you never leave one behind or miss an opportunity to double up with an in-store special. Set your box in the child seat of the shopping cart for easy browsing as you stroll the aisles.

Many Web sites offer coupons for items from groceries and sundries to electronics, books, and flowers. The great thing about cybercoupons is that the Web stores them for you; just print and clip them when it's time to shop, and go!

Sweeping the Kitchen Clean

Keeping the kitchen clean is a daily challenge, but with a few tricks up your sleeve you can create a self-cleaning kitchen. Well . . . almost. Here are some ideas for keeping daily kitchen cleanup organized and easy.

- ✔ **Wash up while you wait for** the water to boil, the chicken to roast, the sauce to reduce. Washing pots and pans as you use them leaves a smaller pile to clean up at the end.

- ✔ **Sweep after every meal,** or at least at the end of each day, so crumbs and fallen food don't get ground into the floor and create a tough cleanup job for later.

- ✔ **Put a plastic mat under the baby's high chair** to catch drips and spills, and then just rinse it off in the sink after feeding time.

✔ **Keep your tools close by.** If you don't have a utility closet in the kitchen for the broom, dustpan, and mop, various organizers are available to hang them from a pantry wall. A first-floor laundry room is another place to put these implements.

Use a plastic dustpan for easy washing when you sweep up something messy.

✔ **Indulge your trashy side.** Most kitchens generate a great deal of garbage, so go ahead and get a nice big, plastic wastebasket that you won't have to empty every five minutes. Keep the wastebasket clean with a plastic garbage bag liner, and watch for spills and mold in the bottom. You can add a second wastebasket alongside to hold bottles, jars, and cans on the way to your recycling bins.

The worst is over. After the kitchen, you just coast down the smooth slope toward total organization. I think now would be a good time to take a break with a cup of tea in your cleaned-up, cooled-down kitchen and contemplate the sweet taste of organizing success.

Chapter 4

Bathe and Beautify: Creating Functional Bathrooms

. . . .

In This Chapter

▶ Improving your grooming with P-L-A-C-E

▶ Defusing bathroom danger zones

▶ Medicine cabinet Rx

▶ Folding and stacking techniques to line up linens

▶ Ending bad bathroom days and empty paper rolls

. . . .

*T*alk about traffic! Some households should have stoplights installed to direct the flow of residents in and out of the bathrooms, and if you have teenagers, you may need a timer too. How can you keep order in a room so public, yet so intimate — the repository of personal-care regimes for every member of the family?

Getting organized in the bathroom can make your mornings go faster and the nightly beeline for bed pick up speed and ease. Perfect your look by arranging all your toiletries within fingertip reach, and polish up your image with well-ordered facilities you can present to guests and visiting repair people without shame. With beautiful bathrooms, organization gets personal.

Where Order Meets Indulgence

Tackle the bathrooms one at a time. You may start with the master bath for inspiration; move on to the family bathroom, where you have your work cut out for you; and finish up with a finesse to the guest baths. In each room, select one section at a time — the countertop, cabinets, drawers, shower and bath, or linen closet and use the five-step P-L-A-C-E system to whip everything into shape and beautify your bathroom space:

- ✔ **Purge:** Toss odds and ends of soap and old, worn, or excess washcloths, towels, sheets, sponges, scrubbers, and loofahs. Eye shadow, lipstick, and blush more than two years old; foundation and powder more than one year old; and eyeliner or mascara more than six months old are neither hygienic nor high quality anymore. So throw them away, along with any personal-care products that you haven't used in the last year. Check dates on medications and dispose of expired ones. Are you using all those travel products collected on your trips? If not, out they go. Old or extra magazines can move to the family room or the trash.

- ✔ **Like with like:** Organize personal-care items and supplies by type in your cabinet drawers, underneath the cabinet, or on linen closet shelves. Shower and bath items can be kept on standing or hanging racks by type or by person. Linen closet items may encompass towels, sheets, medicines, and cleaning supplies, all arranged into like groupings.

✔ **Access:** Place items close to where they're used but out of bathroom users' way, considering safety issues if children are in the house. Countertop items can move to the medicine cabinet, drawers, and under-sink cupboards. Medications need a cool, dry shelf out of the reach of small kids. Extra supplies belong in the linen closet, with the things you use most frequently stored on the middle shelves.

✔ **Contain:** Use baskets, drawers, and/or drawer dividers to contain items by like type: cosmetics, personal-care products, medicines, hair accessories, nail supplies. Put anything that can spill in a leak-proof container. Label containers so it's easy to put things back from where they came.

✔ **Evaluate:** Can you find everything you need to get ready on the sleepiest morning and get to bed on a dog-tired night? Can you shave, style your hair, and apply makeup without taking a step? Is keeping the guest bathroom neat enough for strangers easy? Do you know just where to look when you run out of supplies? Are family members getting in and out of the bathroom fast enough to fit your schedule?

The Organizational Conundrum: Sink and Vanity

Though different people may frequent the master and family bathrooms, you can apply the same logic to both. As always, finish one room before moving on to the next.

If you have a nice, big counter alongside your sink,
count yourself lucky and then count up how much
stuff is cluttering the space. Things left on the countertop look messy, attract dust, and get in the way of
your grooming routines. Here's what can stay out on
your sink or countertop:

- ✔ Hand soap
- ✔ Drinking glasses
- ✔ Box of tissues
- ✔ Clock
- ✔ Radio

 Keep a clock set five minutes fast in all the main
bathrooms to get you moving in the morning.
That you're in on the trick doesn't matter; the
psychology works on sleepyheads.

For the rest of your countertop display, put everything away closest to where you usually access it.
Elegant perfume bottles can grace a bureau in the
bedroom. Shaving supplies go into a cabinet or drawer,
along with cosmetics, hair products, and bath things.
Slip the blow dryer down below, under the sink. Read
on for more details about what goes where — then
come back and clear.

If your bathroom scores low on drawers and you have
a clear corner on the counter, get a set of small countertop drawers to keep your cosmetics and hair
accessories neat and invisible. Figure 4-1 shows this
sleight-of-hand. (Consider safety if children visit this
bathroom.)

Locate your wastebasket near the sink so tossing out
tissues, cotton balls, and razor blades is easy. Plastic
is best for bathroom trash bins; a bag lining keeps the
wastebasket clean and protects it from corrosive
agents such as nail polish remover.

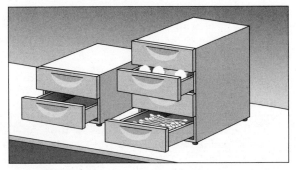

Figure 4-1: Countertop drawers expand your options for cosmetic and accessory storage.

Keep a couple of extra trash bags at the bottom of the wastebasket underneath the open one, so that a replacement is always ready to go.

Medicine cabinet: A misnomer

Whoever named the medicine cabinet must have had excellent health because the medicine cabinet is a terrible place to keep any kind of medication for three reasons:

- ✔ **Safety:** This cabinet is all too accessible to children so even if none live with you but some pass through now and then, keep small stomachs safe from the dangers of all medications, from aspirin to iodine, by storing them on high or locked shelves.

- ✔ **Spoilage:** Heat and humidity from the shower and bath can quickly dissipate the potency of drugs and dietary supplements. Head for drier, cooler ground.

✔ **Accessibility:** Many medications are meant to be taken with food. Unless you eat breakfast in the bathroom, that would put their closest use in the kitchen.

Now that you have the shelves cleared out, here's how to fill them up. Most medicine cabinets have three removable shelves that slide into slots of varying heights. If you have such adjustable architecture, match altitude to access by making the top shelf the highest to fit tall items. That leaves smaller things for the lower shelves, where you can easily spot them, and the shortest for the middle shelf. Here is an example:

✔ **Top shelf:** Hair spray, gel, mousse, shaving cream, aftershave, cologne, antiperspirant, mouthwash

✔ **Middle/shortest:** Toothpaste and toothbrushes, dental floss, razor and refill blades

✔ **Bottom/medium height:** Facial cleansers and lotions, makeup remover and pads, contact lens supplies, eye drops, nasal spray

Do you really want a day's worth of dust on something you put in your mouth? If not, skip the countertop display and hang your toothbrushes from slots in a medicine cabinet shelf instead. Get a different color brush for each bathroom user, and then write down the color code, noting the date the brush was put in service to remind you to replace it six months later. (Get a free one by scheduling a biannual checkup with the dentist.)

Dividing it up: Drawers

Divide your bathroom drawers for fingertip management of the snarl of items commonly found there.

Dividers can range from 2-x-2-inch plastic trays and up to full-drawer sectioned trays. Special cosmetics dividers are designed to hold lipsticks, eye shadows, and so forth; others are sized to hold jewelry. Measure your drawers, count your categories, and shop.

 If you have expensive jewelry, the bathroom is too public a place to store it. Keep your collection on the bedroom bureau or in a fireproof box to maintain peace of mind.

Got just one bathroom drawer? Unless you're a guy, this is probably the place for cosmetics and basic hair tools. Slip in hair accessories if they fit. A rolling cart of drawers is a great addition when you're short on built-ins. It works and it moves. See Table 4-1 for using bathroom drawer space effectively.

Table 4-1	Divine Bathroom Drawers
Drawer	*Items*
Cosmetic center	Foundation, blush, lipstick, eyeliner and shadow, mascara, sponges, brushes, tools
Hair care center	Comb, brush, headbands, barrettes, clips, hairpins, bobby pins, ponytail holders
Jewelry center	Earrings, necklaces, bracelets, watches, pins, jewelry cleaner, polishing cloth

Storing: Under-the-sink cabinets

The space under the sink is a primary storage area for most bathrooms but because shelves are rare in these cabinets, pandemonium is all too common. Solve this problem with space-expanding options:

✔ **Wire-coated shelves** are a quick, no-installation way to add a level to your cabinet. Buy the stackable or multitiered sort if you have lots of vertical space.

✔ **Pullout shelves** slide out of the cabinet to save you from having to reach inside.

✔ **Add a shelf** by buying a piece of wood to size and nailing it in. You may want to make your shelf half the cabinet's depth to leave room for tall things in front.

✔ **Hang a caddy** inside the cabinet door for hair dryers and curling irons. Check out Figure 4-2, and don't forget to account for clearance space.

Photo courtesy of Get Organized!

Figure 4-2: Cabinet door caddy for hair dryer, curling iron, detangler, and brushes.

Next, group your items by like type to create under sink centers and contain them in clear containers or baskets. Table 4-2 shows you how.

Table 4-2	Under Sink Centers
Centers	*Items*
Hair care center	Dryer, curling iron, straightener
Nail care center	Manicure set, nail polish, polish remover, pads
Feminine hygiene center	Tampons, pads, freshness products
Sun protection center	Sunscreen, self-tanner, after-sun moisturizer (move to the linen closet for off-season storage)
Cleaning supply center (if no small children in the house)	Scouring powder, spray cleanser, glass cleaner, disinfectant, toilet bowl cleaner
Plumbing center	Plunger, drain unclogger

If your bathroom serves a large family, get each person a different colored basket to stow personal things in the under-sink cabinet.

Arrange items in the cabinet according to access — closest for use or daily need. That means the hair dryer should be on the side near the electrical outlet and hopefully, your plunger is used infrequently enough that it can go in the back.

Anything that overflows from your bathroom cabinet space can go in the linen closet, if you have one. Coming up short? Try the following:

✔ Try the various shelving or cabinet units that go above the toilet or stand freely on the floor. Some even have wheels for maximum mobility. Skip open-back shelves, which invite things to fall down behind.

✔ Open shelves look cluttered, so contain items when you can — including a toilet paper holder that conceals extra rolls while keeping them close at hand, and a container to hold the toilet brush.

✔ If you like to have reading material within reach, get a basket or magazine rack to hold up to half a dozen magazines. You don't need more here! Save space with containers designed to hold magazines on the bottom and extra toilet paper rolls on top.

Shower and Bath

Who knew keeping clean could be so complicated? If you have the same sort of array of personal care products in your bath or shower and piles of towels all around that I see in my clients' homes, you're well aware of the problem that cleanliness presents: more supplies than space.

Where to hang the towels

Install a towel bar for each person that can hold a washcloth, hand towel, and bath towel. Towel bars are easy to add to a bathroom and can keep towels off the floor and other people from snatching yours. One person can use the shower door bar if you don't have a bath mat hanging there; the back of the door provides another bar-hanging spot. For big families in small bathrooms, double up the hand and bath towel to squeeze two people onto one bar — if you absolutely must. Another space-saving option for a bathroom with four or more users is the towel bar that hangs on the door hinge pictured in Figure 4-3.

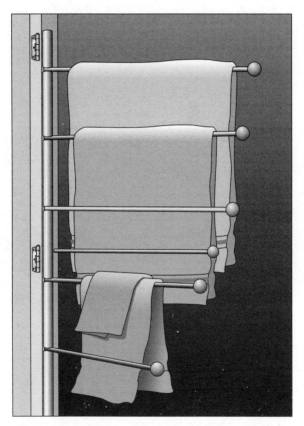

Figure 4-3: This towel bar uses the door hinge for more hanging space.

Put a pair of hooks on the back of the bathroom door to hold clothes and robes. Take down the clothes when you return the robe.

Personal-care products and bath toys

Every shower and bath needs storage systems to hold shampoo, conditioner, skin cleansers, brushes, scrubbers, loofahs, razors, and shaving cream. These can take the form of corner shelves, a rack that hangs from the showerhead, or a tension-rod pole that extends from the top of a bathtub to the ceiling and holds shelves made from wire racking or with holes to let the water drain through (skip the solid, water-collecting ones). Depending upon the size of your family, you can assign shelves by like products or by person.

 Rather bathe than shower? You may want all your supplies on hand without standing up to reach the soap, so get a tray that fits across the width of the tub to hold bath essentials. Some come with a book holder, so you can relax and read without worrying about your best-seller getting wet, as you see in Figure 4-4.

Next take on the rubber duckies: Put kids' bath toys in a mesh bag and hang it from the faucet. If the bath toys don't fit, you have too many . . . unless you have a baby, whose toys are often super-size. Keep those in a dishpan that goes in the under-sink cabinet or floor of the linen closet between baths.

Photo courtesy of Lillian Vernon.

Figure 4-4: Relax and read in a bubble bath.

Hand washables solution: No wet stuff draped on the towels

Doing small hand-wash jobs in the bathroom may be more convenient than to trudge down to the laundry room, but lingerie draped all over is not an attractive sight. Get a closed, nontransparent hamper to hold hand-wash items until washing day, and then dry them on a wire grid rack that hangs over the shower-head, a horizontal rack that sits inside or across the bathtub (this rack is great for sweaters too), or an old-fashioned folding wooden drying rack.

Bathing suits and bras will last longer when washed by hand, particularly the elastic, which the dryer can leave lax and stretched. If you have too many items or too little time to hand-wash, use the delicate wash cycle on the machine and allow to air dry.

Safety and soft, dry landings: The bathroom floors and doors

The bathroom, with all its hard, head-cracking surfaces, is no place to take a spill. Put a no-slip mat or waterproof stickies on the tub or shower floor. Make sure that bath mats or area rugs placed directly on the floor have slip-proof backings (and are machine washable to make your life easier). If your shower doors are crystal clear, congratulations on your good cleaning habits; you may want to put up a couple of stickers to keep people from walking into them like dazed birds.

Don't skip the bath mat just because the bathroom floor is carpeted, because the regular soaking delivered by dripping bodies stepping out of the shower will shorten the life of your carpet. Do you shave your legs or wash your hair in the sink? Stand on a bath mat to keep splashes off the floor.

Closet of All Trades: The Linen Closet

Often viewed as the outfield of the bathroom, the linen closet can accumulate a strange assemblage of clutter but properly organized, this space can outperform its name to serve a variety of purposes. Whether your linen closet is in the bathroom or the hall outside, you should always be able to open the door and easily pull out a clean set of sheets or towels. This is also the place to look for backups of toilet paper or soap bought in bulk (and hopefully on sale!). And what a handy spot for a hammer, the shoe polish, the upstairs cleaning supplies. Everything is possible when you put everything in its place, as follows:

✔ **Purge:** First, pull everything out of your linen closet and toss or donate the excess baggage, including threadbare, stained, and unmatched sheets and towels. One extra set of sheets per bed, plus a set sized for a sofa bed if you have one, will do. A total of two towel sets per person is plenty for basic household needs. Add in up to two sets for guests, four hand towels per guest bathroom, and a beach towel for each family member (four more if guests swim at your house).

Are you awash in minibottles of shampoo and conditioner mooched from hotels? They're not your brand, and the next hotel you visit will provide its own supply. Donate yours to a nursing home, and next time resist the urge to take them home!

✔ **Sort and sift:** Select the items that are best stored in the linen closet and group them by like type for easy access.

The linen closet may seem like an unlikely spot for tools but do you really want to run down to the basement every time you want to hang a picture or open a pipe? Keep a small toolkit in the linen closet for jobs in this part of the house.

✔ **Assign space:** Think high-low. Store items that are seldom used or dangerous to children on the highest shelves, small things that are hard to spot at eye level, and light but big items below. For higher-middle shelves, think personal-care items, first aid kit, shoe care, cleaning supplies, toolbox. The middle-lower shelves can be used for bed and bath linens while the bottom shelves/floor can accommodate bath and facial tissue, extra blankets, trash bags, travel cosmetic/shaving kits, and a sick bucket.

✔ **Group and stack:** If jamming your clean sheets onto the shelf is something like pushing your way onto a New York subway car, it's time to clean up your act. The right folding technique can stack your sheets up neatly with an easy visual ID of what's what. There may not be as many ways to store a towel as there are shoes, but there are at least two: folding and rolling.

Next are personal-care items and cleaning supplies: Contain items in clear or different colored baskets, grouped by like type, and make it easy (or difficult for kids) to access what you need. Pullout drawers that sit on the shelf can help. Add labels so that one look takes you to your target.

The best spot for extra blankets is in the bedroom, closest to their use. If you don't have room there, use a bottom shelf of the linen closet, because blankets are light and easy to lift.

If you travel frequently, keep a shaving or cosmetic kit always packed with sample-size products and ready to go. Replenish your supplies as you return from each trip.

First aid center: Safety first

A complete first aid center can be a quick, sometimes critical help for illnesses and injuries, but many of its contents can be poisonous or dangerous to small children. Prevent your own first aid emergency by keeping your kit on a high linen closet shelf.

The components of a well-stocked first aid center may include adhesive bandages, gauze pads and adhesive tape, elastic bandage, arm sling, ice bag, heating pad, antibiotic ointment, muscle sprain cream, rubbing alcohol, hydrogen peroxide, calamine lotion, sunburn products, thermometer, scissors, tweezers, aspirin (ibuprofen/acetaminophen), antihistamines, loperamide, bismuth, syrup of ipecac, and prescription insect bite or food allergy kits.

The Half or Guest Bath

A half bath is really a half room (which luckily presents less of a logistical problem). Bath math dictates that you can have only half the stuff in a guest bath as in a main bathroom:

- ✔ **Sink and counter:** Maximize the aesthetics of the guest bath by keeping only what visitors may need out on the countertop. Sink and counter items may include a decorative pump-style bottle of liquid soap so that guests don't have to share germs, a box of tissues, a bottle of hand lotion, and some small paper cups, preferably in a wall-mounted dispenser.

- ✔ **Towel bar:** Hang at least two hand towels in the guest bath. If your family uses these frequently and you like things fancy, keep a separate stack of elegant towels on the sink for visitors.

✔ **Under-the-sink cabinet:** This is the spot for hiding away necessities and supplies, such as an extra package of toilet paper, box of tissues, bottle of hand soap, and feminine hygiene supplies. Some cleaning supplies to have here are sponges, scouring powder, spray cleanser, glass cleaner, toilet bowl cleaner, and a plunger.

✔ **Reading material:** Keep magazines neat with a small stand and don't overfill.

Now you're all cleaned up in your cleanup centers. Doesn't your bathroom feel beautifully pristine?

I'm out of what?

The most important item in any guest bathroom is toilet paper. While family members may be quick to pipe up when the roll runs out, guests usually won't, so spare everybody the embarrassment by keeping some backup paper in plain sight. Simply place a spare roll on top of the tank, or go upscale with a decorative container designed to hold three to four rolls on the floor.

Chapter 5

The Hangout Spot: The Family and Media Room

. . . .

In This Chapter

▶ Creating a space for pure comfort

▶ Enlightening your entertainment center

▶ How to be a well-ordered bookworm

▶ Managing magazines with expertise

▶ Better family relations through organization

. . . .

*A*h, home at last. You kick back on the couch, crank up the DVD player, and prepare to lose yourself in your favorite film. But the DVD in the case marked *Casablanca* seems to be projecting singing dinosaurs onto the screen — not at all the thing for your tension headache — the remote is nowhere to be found, and is that an old pizza box peeking out from under that pile of magazines?

The model family room is comfort defined, a casual place for letting it all hang out. But you can't relax among piles or while hunting for the remote control or digging through a stack of Rolling Stones CDs in search of some soothing Bach. Promote family harmony with a well-organized family room, and watch your recreation quotient rise.

How can you let everyone do their own thing in the family room, yet still have some semblance of order? Teach all the room's occupants the power of the principles of P-L-A-C-E:

✔ **Purge:** Toss any malfunctioning, obsolete, or duplicate equipment; videos and DVDs you no longer watch, music nobody listens to anymore, and books you won't read again; and old magazines, including back issues you haven't read.

✔ **Like with like:** Arrange tapes and discs by format and category, books by fiction/nonfiction and category, and photos by date in boxes or into albums or frames. Group remote controls together with a remote caddy.

✔ **Access:** Arrange furniture for conversation, watching television, and listening to music. Place home-entertainment equipment in a media unit designed to accommodate equipment and make connections easy. In the bookcase, place heavier books on lower shelves and lighter ones higher up.

✔ **Contain:** Store and contain tapes and discs in drawers, shelves, or storage units, books in the bookcase, current magazines in a rack, and games, toys, photos, and collections in closed shelves and drawers or the playroom or basement.

✔ **Evaluate:** Can you straggle into this room after a long, hard day and quickly access the recreation you crave? Is the room so comfortable and peaceful that you sometimes fall asleep in your chair? Do the members of your family get along, find what they need, and have fun when they're here?

Casually Neat Is Not a Contradiction

Though the family room is a great place to forget formality, that doesn't mean order can go out the window too. Neatness counts extra in this room because it's usually the most lived-in. The den's image permeates the consciousness of your home's inhabitants. Wouldn't you like that picture to be one of peace?

Furnish the family room with comfort in mind. Like to get lazy? Indulge in a reclining chair with a built-in or separate footstool. Or go overstuffed with big, comfy armchairs. A nice, long couch can accommodate the whole family at movie-watching time; point the couch toward the screen and angle chairs on either side so you can talk or watch. Add enough end tables to hold drinks, and double up their use with drawers and shelves underneath for photos, coin and stamp collections, games, and toys. Store some TV trays or lap trays in the closet if you're inclined to have snacks or casual meals here.

Fun or Frustrating: The Media Center

A media unit is a must to provide easy access to a full complement of equipment — television, VCR or DVD player, and stereo system. Designed to shelve the

various components of your system and accommodate all the connecting cables, media units also have
drawers to store manuals, program guides, cleaning
kits, extra cables, tapes, DVDs, and CDs. Built-in units
offer the best stability, but you can also buy a freestanding system. If you must make do with a bookcase, drill holes in the back for cables and cords. Use
extra shelf space and shelf-top organizers to store
CDs, DVDs, and tapes.

Some people call this the Information Age, but I sus-
pect it's really the Equipment Age — and if you accu-
mulated an epoch's worth of unused entertainment
equipment, clear the stuff out. The eight-track tape
deck? History! The skipping CD player you keep thinking you'll take in for service? Either do it or give it
away. Your little tabletop TV is shamed by the new
big-screen model you just installed. Move the smaller
version to the kitchen or call a charity for pickup.

Does your remote control like to play hide and seek
between the couch cushions? Take control with a
caddy that has a place for your remote unit and
current program guide. You can even attach it to your
favorite easy chair. See Figure 5-1 for ways to take
control of your controls. If you have several remotes
for different equipment, a universal unit can combine
them all into one.

Fight media burnout with a scheme to make home
entertainment easy again. Four easy steps can
enlighten your entertainment collection and put
hours of fun at your fingertips:

Figure 5-1: Remote control caddy stands keep you in command.

1. **Purge and sort.** Gather the family and go through all your tapes and discs, purging everything that no one's watched or listened to for a year. Cries of extreme sentimental value can be accommodated, but remember that you can always rent movies as well as borrow movies and music from the library. As you go, sort items by like format.

If your cast-off CDs still have popular appeal, take them to a used CD store for cash. You can also donate CDs and commercial videos and audiotapes to a library or school.

2. **Categorize.** Group like items by genre or category. Alphabetize titles within each category. Using the artist's or composer's name for music and the show name for DVDs is usually the easiest method.

   Audio categories may include classical, jazz, rock/pop, rhythm and blues/soul, rap/hip hop, blues, country, musicals/soundtracks, world/folk, children's, and books on tape. For video, consider categorizing by movies (subdivided into drama, comedy, musicals, and foreign if you have a lot), television shows, entertainment (concerts, magic shows), children's, sports, exercise, how-to, and home videos.

3. **Position for access and contain.** Devise your optimal storage strategy by comparing your space to the number of pieces you need to store in each format and identifying where you can most easily reach. Containing options for your audiovisual software include drawers in the media unit, in a freestanding unit, or under tables; bookcase or wall shelves; spinning turntables; and freestanding towers.

   Figure 5-2 illustrates one idea for media storage. Whatever you choose, make sure you can keep all the pieces in a given format together.

4. **Identify your media. Create a computer list — a database, spreadsheet, or even just a word-processing document — of everything in your collection by category.** Keep an updated printout in a drawer of your media center as an easy-browsing menu.

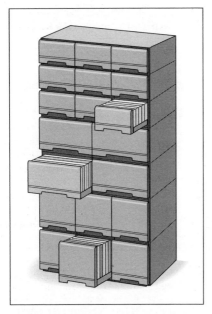

Figure 5-2: Enlightened entertainment storage options include stackable drawers.

The Computer Equation

In homes without an office, the family room may be the only place to put a computer. The downside of this strategy is that one family member may want to watch a movie or listen to mind-numbing heavy metal music while another is trying to do homework or balance the checkbook on the computer. Rules may need to be set — such as homework assignments come first — and having a spare TV in another room can help ease their enforcement.

If you don't like the look of a computer in your family room, you can buy an armoire designed to keep it under cover.

Managing Your Precious Moments: Photographs

The cherished memories in your photo collection can become a clutter problem fast. Shutterbugs can bene-fit from a few friendly photo tips. First, purge the lemons: There's no prize for hanging on to bad pic-tures, so give them the boot. See? You can reinvent the past. After you've picked through and found all of the ones that are blurry, too far away, or where the subject's eyes are shut, you can manage the ones that are worth keeping efficiently by doing the following:

- ✔ **Label and date.** Match the moment to the memory by labeling and dating each envelope as you get it back from the developer. If your camera doesn't have a date stamp, date the backs of pictures too, and note the names of non-immediate family members for when memory starts to fade. Never use markers, which can bleed; art stores sell special blue pen-cils for writing on the backs of photos.

- ✔ **Display.** What's the point of photos you never look at? Enjoy your pictures by putting them in frames or a photo album or scrapbook right away, or make a date with yourself to do it at least once a year (more if you're a frequent pho-tographer). Some frames hold several pictures so that you can make your own collage. Have fun creating family history collages, and then hang them in the hall so everyone can remem-ber where they came from.

✔ **Scrapbooks.** Assembling a scrapbook is a great family project. Choose a snowy or rainy day, or if your kids are in college, steal a few hours over break. Check out scrapbook stores chock full of things to jazz up your book, from funny quotes to fancy borders and stickers. If you prefer to seek professional help, there are specialists who teach design ideas and let you make multiple visits to their facility for advice and the camaraderie of other scrapbook creators.

✔ **Store safely.** Preserve your photos by keeping them in acid-free boxes or albums made with acid-free paper. Shoebox living can age photos fast.

Books and Bookshelves: The Library

I know you're not a librarian, and it probably shows. You don't have to know the Dewey decimal system to bring order to your reading matter, though. Here's how to lighten up the library. Go through your books and purge all the dinosaurs, which include the following:

✔ Outdated or irrelevant reference books (such as the college guide if all of your kids have graduated)

✔ Novels you won't read again (who reads anything twice anymore?)

✔ Outgrown children's books

✔ Old textbooks

✔ Anything you don't expect to open in the next year (unless it's a classic). Information is now easy to access and quick to change, so don't clutter your bookcase with yesterday's news.

Donate unwanted books to a library, school, or senior home, or sell your best titles to a used bookstore.

Arrange your books on the shelves by category, grouping like with like. For fiction, you can categorize by novels, short stories, plays, and children's books. Good nonfiction categories include reference (dictionaries, encyclopedias, thesaurus), biography, history, religion, English, arts, science, math, health/medicine, crafts/hobbies, travel, and photo albums, scrapbooks, and yearbooks. Within each category, alphabetize your books by author. Ease access and be kind to your case by keeping heavier books (think reference) on the bottom shelves and lighter ones (paperback novels) on top. Resist the urge to stack books two rows deep, as you may never see the ones in back.

If you purged and still have more books than shelf space, it's time for a new bookcase. Look for one with adjustable shelves so you can change the height to suit hard covers or paperbacks. Measure your space before shopping to be sure your dimensions match. Twelve inches depth is plenty of room.

Clutter or Current: Magazines

Magazines come out every week or month for a reason: You're supposed to read them now and move on. Keep only the current issues of magazines and purge the rest — yes, even if you haven't read them. If you later discover that you missed the only tell-all interview with your favorite movie star ever printed, you can find it at the library. (Schools sometimes use old magazines for various projects, if you'd rather donate than toss.) Assess your subscription portfolio.

Do you really need everything you receive? Is there a magazine you haven't gotten to for the last three issues? Are you reading some of them online? Do you subscribe to a weekly news magazine simply because you think you should only to have it lie around unopened week after week? Are you tired of some of the titles you've been receiving for years? Call to cancel any superfluous subscriptions.

The whole magazine: Rack 'em

Contain your current magazine issues in a rack. As each new issue arrives, rack it up and discard the previous one. No doubling up.

 You can use your magazine rack to store current catalogs too. The same rule applies: Toss out the old as you rack up the new. If you receive catalogs you don't want, call and ask to be removed from the mailing list.

Articles: File 'em

For good magazine management, mark the table of contents of each issue as you get it and tear out any articles you want to read. (If you're sharing with others or like to browse the ads, you can pull the articles when the time comes to throw the magazine away instead.) Staple each article together and place it in a To Read file that you can take along on commutes, to the doctor's office, and so on.

Some people are prone to collect magazines that cover their profession or hobby to serve as a reference. If you're not referring to back issues more than once or twice a year, you're better off tossing them and looking up information at the library or on the

Internet as needed. However, if you find yourself flipping through your old magazines a few times a month, they may qualify as a viable resource. You can retrieve information fastest by tearing out articles that interest you and filing them by subject, so when you want to know if you should use the wedge or the five iron to get out of a sand trap, you need only pull out the folder labeled "Golf — Sand Trap" rather than pore through three years of your favorite golf magazine indexes. If you must save whole magazines, keep no more than a few years' worth (after that the articles probably repeat) and store them in chronological order, grouped by year in magazine holders that sit on the bookshelf. Label each holder with the magazine title and issue dates.

Games, Toys, and Collections

A family that plays together stays together, but how do you keep your fun neat? Most families accumulate quite a few games, toys, and collections in the course of having fun. I'm all in favor of being fully equipped to play, and ask only that you give all your playthings a place.

Keeping games fun (and organized!)

If the family room is your prime game-playing area, buy a closed cabinet that can contain everything behind doors. A bookshelf is a less scenic alternative. Infrequent gamers or those just as likely to play in another room may put your gaming center in the playroom, basement, or hall closet, keeping just a couple of family favorites — cards, checkers — in a drawer in the den.

Keep electronic games by the TV on which they're played in clear storage boxes or special units designed to hold them, such as the one in Figure 5-3.

Photo courtesy of Lillian Vernon.

Figure 5-3: Sleek storage for electronic games.

The toy crate

Toys need to be mobile when you have toddlers so that you can keep the kids amused as you herd them around the house under your watchful eye. While that's the case, keep a crate of toys in the family room so you don't have to chase up and down the stairs in search of a bear or truck. When the children are old enough to play in the playroom or their bedrooms without supervision, move the toys and eliminate the crate.

Stamps, coins, shot glasses, and spoons: Collections

Collectors of coins, stamps, shot glasses, and such tend to enjoy showing off, and the den is a good place for their displays. Whether you arrange your collection on a shelf, in a shadow box, or in a hanging wall display, make sure everything is easy to see — that is, well-spaced and at the right height. You don't want to hang your rare coins so high that no one can read the years. A glass enclosure can help preserve a valuable collection. Many collectors' clubs offer complete guidelines for storing and protecting your precious goods. If your collection is of less visual than personal interest, it may belong in a bedroom instead.

Chapter 6

Organizing for Fun: The Playroom

· ·

In This Chapter

▶ Setting the stage for creativity

▶ Creating play centers for one-stop fun

▶ Purging the playroom without tears

▶ Advanced toy management

▶ Crafting art supply tricks

▶ Making a multigenerational playroom

· ·

*P*lay is important to people of all ages, but for children, amusement is a 24/7 job. The mess that can come from hard-core fun makes a separate room for play a great plan. Not only does a playroom keep toys, crafts, and games out from underfoot in the rest of the house, but a playroom also provides young minds with a special place to let their imaginations soar.

Children learn as they play. Show your kids how to keep the playroom clean and organized, and you'll give them a powerful tool for productivity and clear thinking that can last a lifetime. P-L-A-C-E provides the framework for your cleaned-up playroom. Here is how you employ it:

✔ **Purge:** Throw away or donate outgrown, unused, and broken toys, including games and puzzles with missing pieces. Pitch old or duplicate-color crayons, dried-out markers, paints, and glue.

✔ **Like with like:** Put items into play centers — toddlers, dress-up, playing school, and so on. Place game pieces and puzzles into resealable bags and onto shelves. Arrange books by category.

✔ **Access:** Put all large equipment, such as indoor slides or train displays, at one end of the room, and potentially dangerous or messy art and craft supplies in a childproof cabinet near their use. Keep small toys such as marbles and doll accessories higher up, out of the reach of smaller children who can choke on them.

✔ **Contain:** Place toys into containers by type and age group or individual. Add labels for quick identification and to help younger children learn to read. Put art and craft supplies into separate containers or rolling carts.

✔ **Evaluate:** Do children and adults feel free to play, create, and make believe in this room? Can children find and put away their own toys? Do games and puzzles always have all their pieces in place? Do you feel safe leaving your children here unsupervised? Is there a space for every sort of fun your family likes?

Positioning the Play Centers

The playroom can be conducive to creativity and to cleaning up afterward. Much of the action in this room takes place on the floor, so tackle that first and work your way up. A nice, soft carpet is great for ground-based games and play, but carpeting can also take a beating from art supplies and spills. My favorite solution is indoor/outdoor carpeting, which I initially installed with an eye toward a possible flood in our basement playroom, but I quickly discovered two additional perks: Accidents can be vacuumed up or washed away with soap and water in a flash, and toys are easily pushed across the flat pile into piles for quick pickups. Genius!

Now for the fun part: creating your worlds of play. You know how a grocery store stocks the pastas next to the sauces so you can pick up dinner all in one aisle? You can do the same in the playroom, setting up centers for various activities and age groups that make each spot a different adventure. Play centers are actually nothing more than an imaginative version of fingertip management and access, putting fun within easy reach.

One play center might include toddler toys, while another part of the room is set up to play school. The dress-up center can contain clothes and a mirror for showing them off; the building center could be stocked with builder sets; and the music center gathers together instruments, CDs, and players. If you have big equipment such as a slide or trampoline, establish an action center at one end of the room.

Your play center arrangements may need to change with your children's interests and ages. Freshening up the playroom with periodic repositioning keeps everyone interested in its organization, and provides an excellent opportunity to purge the cast-offs as you go.

How to Be a Senior Toy Manager

If you've been there, you know: Toy management is serious business. Those who do manage toys well ought to receive an honorable degree, acknowledging the advanced techniques required to keep order between fun-loving young souls and the adults who love to lavish them with gifts. The good news is that once you master the three key toy-management principles, you can keep your playroom and its players on track without panicking every time the grandparents show up with *presents*.

The three steps to advanced toy management are

1. **Purge:** In today's world, many kids are in total toy overload. To adults, toys can come to represent both love and money spent, and tossing toys may be even harder for mom than daughter. But as sentimental as each gift from loving parents, doting grandparents, and adoring aunts and uncles may be, kids outgrow toys quickly and can only play with so many current favorites at once. Keeping extra or obsolete toys encourages bad habits and wastes space — which itself is a critical part of the creativity equation. So take the plunge. Purge your playroom today.

   Depending upon your children's ages and the toys involved, you may choose to approach the task with each child individually, or do the whole family in one fell swoop. Sort toys and games by type, directing the cast-offs to trash, donation, and garage sale piles as you go.

 Purging your playroom can be approached gently. Never make children get rid of toys before they're ready, but do look for staged compromises that respect a child's feelings while also helping children form a healthy relationship with material things.

2. **Contain:** Enclosing toys in containers keeps them from becoming clutter and accustoms kids to looking for things in their place and putting their toys back in the appropriate container later. Match the container to the type of toy and age of the users. Colored open crates can hold large toys for small toddlers. Use a different color for each type of toy — blocks, cars, dolls, animals. Clear, pullout drawers suit smaller items and make seeing what's inside easy at play and cleanup time. Preschoolers love 'em. Closed wicker baskets or chests are an attractive way to house dolls and doll clothes. Containers with tight-fitting lids keep smaller children out of older children's toys, so that Judy can keep her beloved doll accessories in the playroom without worrying that little Phillip may stop by and swallow a tiny high-heeled shoe.

Arrange your containers in cabinets or on wall shelves, keeping crayons, board games, and craft supplies up high and toddler-friendly toys closer to the floor.

Go for closed: Look for full backs and sides on all of your playroom containers and shelving. Small toys and game and puzzle pieces have a way of slipping through cracks into irretrievable spots.

3. **Rotate:** Even after your purge, you'll probably have more toys than your children can play with at once. Absence makes the heart grow fonder, so prolong the appeal of toys and games by rotating your active stock. To establish a toy rotation, divide each toy type into a few different groups, so that the sum of one group from each type will leave your playroom well-stocked. Box up the remaining groups by set, label each one with a toy rotation number, and store in the basement or attic far from inquiring eyes.

When your kids start to tire of the playroom repertoire, it's time for the big switcheroo. You can make a big deal of the switch, enlisting kids to pack up old toys before bringing on the new batch, or make the change yourself quietly one night. Surprise! Rotations also provide a good time to trim down the collection. Are all the toys you'll pack up still on the "A" list? Toss or donate the C's through Z's — but remember that a little time away can reestablish the luster of many a B.

No cutting corners: Storing games

One nice thing about games is that they come in their own box, but boy, do those boxes break fast, especially the corners. Mend breaks with masking tape applied to the inside of the box, which can keep the box looking nice and improve your chances of getting the game out and put away without pieces all over the floor.

Speaking of pieces, protect your peace of mind by zipping them into resealable bags. This makes cleanup far easier when the box takes a tumble. Use the slide type of closure for easy access to younger kids' games and a pressure closure for those you might want to keep little ones out of.

 Some games have paper books that are necessary to play the game. If the game's a family favorite, extend the life of the book by covering the pages with clear contact paper.

Learn to read while you play with labels

Even toy retrieval can become a reading experience when you label toy containers with their contents. Tommy may not know the word "cars" on sight, but show him that his toy hot rod goes in the drawer with those four letters on the front and watch his cognitive wheels start to turn.

Make the reading lesson easier by using both upper and lowercase letters in your labels. Small letters, with their distinct shapes and heights, are easier to recognize than all caps. I recommend a label maker, which is relatively cheap (less than $50), for the job and the resulting labels look much better than masking tape or a curling computer label, and they're washable. With your help, your preschoolers may like punching out a label or two for themselves.

Getting it together: Puzzles

You can never put all the pieces of a puzzle together if some have gone missing, so use a system to keep them in their place:

> ✔ As soon as you bring a puzzle home, mark the back of each piece with the puzzle's name or a number, for example, "Farmhouse" or "23." If you use a number code, write the number on the puzzle box. Now if a piece pops up somewhere else, you know just where to put the piece back.

✔ Put puzzle pieces into a resealable bag inside the box to prevent spills.

✔ Devote a card or snack table to the puzzle for as long as you work on it. Place the table in a corner to keep it from getting knocked over or interfering with other activities.

The Reading Center: Children's Books

Playrooms are often freewheeling places — not the best environment for a reading center, so I generally recommend keeping most children's books in bedrooms or the library or family room. However, the playroom is the right room for activity, art, and craft books, and you may put the rest of your collection here if you don't have space elsewhere or if the playroom is your prime reading spot. Depending upon how many books you have, use a small freestanding bookcase or larger wall unit to put them into place. If you keep reading books here, put older children's books higher up so younger siblings won't access and destroy them, and devote the lower shelves to toddler favorites. Shelve books by like category: activity, reference, fiction or stories, fairy tales, religious books, and so on. See Chapter 5 for more on categorizing and shelving a library.

Saving for a sentimental journey

Popular toys change at the speed of light. My girls grew up with toys that hadn't been invented in my day and contemporary kids can't even recognize. As a current mom of college students, I'm unfamiliar with today's toys. My point: Many toys are trendy, and it's generally best to get rid of them as they pass out of the spotlight.

Still, some toys are evergreens for educational or sentimental reasons, and to keep a few for the grandchildren is okay. I chose three boxes to hang onto from my children's younger days, filled with some dolls, a set of 2-inch-high animal families that's been off the market for years, and basic building blocks that can enable the construction of any dream, from houses to airports, fire stations, and entire towns. The dolls may be the most lasting reminder of my limited skills as a seamstress. I labored over making them new outfits, and hoped that someday my grandchildren may enjoy playing with their mothers' dolls and laughing at their grandmother's stitches. As for the mini animals, when my girls were young there was a television show that taught life lessons through families of rabbits, bears, and raccoons. I made up a lot of stories voiced through the mouths of these guys, and plan to tell new ones the soonest chance I get.

So my sentimental savers are destined to be grandma's toys, a select and special few that meet my own needs while leaving my children the space to create their own memories with a new generation. When it comes to sentiment, selectivity is key.

The Art of Organizing Arts 'n' Crafts

Setting up an arts and crafts area for kids is like arranging an adult workshop or hobby area, while accounting for safety issues and a lot more messes.

First, create the art center. Remind yourself that if there's a nice carpet on the floor, you may want to recarpet with indoor/outdoor material, use a drop cloth, or relegate activities involving clay, paints, markers, or glue to the kitchen. Keep all messy supplies in a childproof cabinet closest to their use.

If you don't have a mess-proof floor in the art center or want to double up your cooking with supervising an arts-and-craft session, set up your craft station in the kitchen, storing supplies in a high or locked cabinet and using the kitchen table for a worktable. You can knock off a stew or sauce while they stamp, paint, or glue, and everyone can have something to show at the end.

By the way, buy washable markers, paints, and glue while kids are young enough to consider the world and the walls their canvas. For a worktable in the playroom, a kitchen cast-off fills the bill. Laminated tops are easiest to clean up, while wood may get wrecked and stained by paints and crayons, but maybe you don't care.

Next, stock your supplies. As always, art supplies can be accessible close to the worktable, with like items together and everything contained in dividers or other containers in drawers or on shelves. An old dresser may be put to use for craft supply storage. Playrooms have lots of craft stuff and art supplies, so here are some ways to consolidate and store all of those supplies for those future creations:

- ✔ **Crayons:** Save new, intact boxes of crayons for school and collect the rest in a covered plastic box or metal tin at home. Metal won't get as marked up as plastic.

- ✔ **Pencils, pens, markers, scissors:** Use narrow plastic divider trays, preferably inside a drawer to prevent a spill.

- ✔ **Rubber stamps:** Store them in their original cases or spread on a piece of paper. Stamping the paper with the design can help you find the stamp you want.

- ✔ **Paints:** Stack watercolors in their own containers, organize others into plastic trays.

- ✔ **Glues:** Group together in a plastic tray.

- ✔ **Paper:** If you have several types (white, construction, drawing, and so on), use an office sort tray.

- ✔ **Beads:** Corral beads into containers specially designed to separate them by type.

Attention kids and parents everywhere: Crayons aren't used up just because you wore them down to the paper. Buy a crayon sharpener to keep a slim tip on your crayons and enjoy their full life span. Got more crayons than you can use? Day care centers are always happy for the donation.

Rec Room and Playroom Combo: All-Ages Fun!

We all need to play, and doubling up the playroom as a recreation and relaxation room for teenagers and adults can be a boon to family togetherness — if you have the space to let everyone do their thing. Keep centers in mind so that you can cohabitate playfully and peacefully. Add an adult sitting area with a couch, some comfy chairs, and perhaps a media center and/or library. Big games such as pool or ping-pong can go into their own game center away from the sitting area so the action doesn't detract from anyone's relaxation factor. Point the couch and chairs toward the kids' play areas, and you can keep a watchful eye while you enjoy your book or show.

Cleaning up your act

The playroom may be the space with the shortest organizational attention span in the house. Whatever the project or game, every session here needs to routinely end with cleanup time. From the moment your children can walk, show them not to walk out of the room until everything is put away. The payoff? Fun and easy play tomorrow, without a mess to wade through on the way.

Kid-friendly ways to clean up your act include the following:

✔ Clean up with them when the kids are young.

✔ Invite older children to think up better ways to straighten up and systematize the playroom. Throw down the gauntlet anew every year.

✔ Turn on special cleanup music and challenge everyone to be done by the time the song is over.

✔ Set a good example yourself in other areas of the house. Getting organized in the playroom can make fun come naturally for all — so forget your excuses and get playing with everything in its place!

Chapter 7

Lightening Your Load: The Laundry and Utility Room

. . . .

In This Chapter

▶ Preventing nothing-to-wear mornings

▶ Rising above piles with savvy sorting secrets

▶ How to shrink anything — or not

▶ Clutter-taming caddies and drying racks

▶ Setting up a mess-free mudroom

. . . .

*A*ir the dirty laundry: You probably spend far more time than you like in an overheated room that smells like lint in a losing battle to keep your closets stocked with clean clothes. How can you ever win?

Weary washers of the world take heart. Getting organized in the laundry room can take a big load off your mind and lighten your burden of chores. Whether you have the luxury of your very own laundry room (bet you never thought of it that way), share a laundry room with fellow apartment dwellers, or lug your duds to the public laundromat, a lean-and-mean approach to keeping your clothes clean can enhance both your look and your life.

The laundry room is a place for making things clean, so put everything into P-L-A-C-E by applying those five organizing principles:

- ✔ **Purge:** Toss out old laundry supplies; bent, mis-shapen, or excess hangers; worn or torn dust rags; and any dried-up or old craft or holiday supplies in your utility center. If you have return/repair items you haven't dealt with in a year, let them go now.

- ✔ **Like with like:** Put laundry supplies together by type above, next to, or between the machines, right where you use them.

- ✔ **Access:** Keep hampers in bedroom closets to collect dirty laundry at the source. In the laundry room, create a sorting center, drying center, ironing center, and utility center to complete each task in one spot.

- ✔ **Contain:** Keep laundry supplies in cabinets or shelving units near the machines. Place the ironing tools in an organizer on the wall or door. Put craft supplies in clear containers and label them for easy access.

- ✔ **Evaluate:** Do dirty clothes easily make their way into the right load? Can you reach all the laundry supplies while standing at the machine? Can you sort clean clothes without taking a step? Is getting dirty clothes in and clean clothes out of the laundry and helping with a weekly load easy for household members? Does working in this room make you feel like a paragon of efficiency, or an underpaid drudge?

Doing the Laundry Where You Live

Most of us don't have a choice in the matter, but if you do, here's my maxim: Do the laundry where you live. Whoever thought of putting laundry rooms in the basement, two floors away from where we take off dirty clothes and put on clean ones, was clearly unacquainted with the principle of fingertip management. The closer you can locate the laundry to your bedrooms the better, so you who have first- or second-floor facilities can count yourselves blessed. The rest of you, whether descending to the basement or heading out of the house, can consider it extra calories burned or a social break.

No matter where you do your laundry, you can save time and steps by keeping a hamper for dirty clothes in each bedroom, where clothes can be deposited as each person undresses. Look for vented hampers that let clothes breathe, and if there's a lot of ground to cover between the closet and the washing machine, why not get one with wheels on the bottom so you can roll instead of carrying? Figure 7-1 shows this easy-handling hamper.

Photo courtesy of Get Organized!.

Figure 7-1: Lighten your load with a rolling laundry hamper.

Hallway facilities

Hallway washer-dryer setups usually accommodate just the machines and a few cabinets or shelves above. Forget about spreading out a bunch of laundry baskets. At best you can stow baskets on top of the machines while the laundry is inside; at worst — if the machines themselves are stacked — the baskets must be stored in the bedroom at all times. You also

have limited space for storing supplies, sorting, and
air-drying — but read on for tips about facilitating
each of these tasks.

 If you can, enclosing hallway laundry facilities
behind doors is best. Keep them closed so you
don't have to look at the machines and think
about your dirty laundry every time you walk by.

The laundry room

A dedicated laundry room provides the space you
need to get the job done with ease, if you arrange the
room well and refrain from filling it up with other stuff.

To give everyone easy access to supplies and key
areas for doing laundry, divide the laundry area into
the following centers:

- ✔ Sorting center for dirty and clean clothes
- ✔ Drying center
- ✔ Ironing center

 If you have a laundry chute, put an 18-gallon garbage can underneath to catch clothes easily and
prevent having to pick up the overflows and
misses that shallow baskets can cause. You can
use a low shelf or table to position the can as
close to the chute as possible.

A well-stocked laundry room can conquer many a
stain and ensure you always have the right product
for the job. But a box of detergent you can't find has
zero cleaning power, and shuffling through bottles
when you have a big pile of dirty clothes staring you
down can raise your irritation quotient fast. The right
storage systems can help you whip your supplies into
place and lose the laundry blues. The following can
make laundry simple:

✔ **Built-in shelves above the machines:** A couple of midlevel shelves above your washer and dryer can contain your detergent and fabric softener at closest possible use. Solid shelving is better than wire racks because the smooth surface provides better balance to small containers and prevents any drips or leaks from oozing down behind the machines. The disadvantage of shelving is that you have to look at everything, which isn't as aesthetic as hiding things away.

If you store cleaning or dusting rags on shelves, place them in a container so they don't ruin your view or fall through wire racks.

✔ **Built-in cabinets above the machines:** These offer the same ease of access as shelves. You do lose a little time opening the doors to locate and reach for an item or take inventory, but you have the added advantage of concealing the contents.

✔ **Freestanding shelves or cabinets above or next to the machines:** If you don't have built-ins and would rather not install cabinets yourself, you can purchase freestanding units that rise above the machines or stand along the wall.

✔ **Caddies next to or between machines:** From rolling wire rack shelves to slim towers that slip between the washer and dryer, there's a laundry caddy to suit every need. Look for one that works with your layout and can hold all your supplies in one place. Figure 7-2 presents a possibility.

Group supplies by type, so that all the detergents and bleaches go together close by the washing machine with stain treatments alongside. If you treat stains in a sink or on a worktable, then put your antistain products near there. The fabric softener can sit near the dryer, so everything has its own slot and retrieving and putting away is easy.

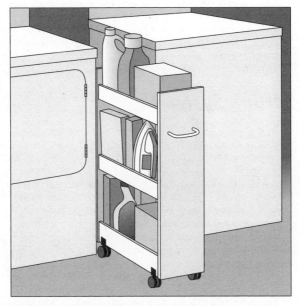

Figure 7-2: If you're short on space, this skinny caddy helps keep laundry supplies in place between the machines.

Apartment laundry rooms and public laundromats

Organizing your laundry is all the more important if your residence has no laundry facilities. Designate a spot — under the kitchen or bathroom sink, in the linen closet, utility closet, or pantry, or in a back hall — to store all your supplies and a stash of quarters. Use a rolling hamper and portable supply caddy to ease transport.

Keep at least enough quarters on hand to wash and dry all the loads you typically do in a session. Whether you buy a roll of quarters at the bank or accumulate change in a jar, you can cut out hustling for coins from your chore.

Sorting Systems

Sorting, the first step to laundry success, can be as simple or as complicated as your clothes collection requires.

A well-organized sorting system can help you rise above those piles on the floor and keep each load neat and contained. Sorting solutions on the market include a set of canvas bags hanging from a frame with a hinge-top table above for folding (see Figure 7-3), sliding baskets set into a standing frame to maximize your vertical space, and the old-fashioned method of baskets set on a table.

To sort clothes the savvy way, do the following:

1. **The dry and the wet:** First filter out garments bound for the dry cleaners before garments go anywhere, preferably in the bedroom. Designate a separate hamper or hanging spot in the closet for items to take to the cleaners.

   The chemicals used in dry cleaning are tough on fabric, so the less often you take clothes to the cleaners, the longer they last. Once or twice a season is probably enough for all but the most-frequently worn items.

Photo courtesy of Get Organized!.

Figure 7-3: A laundry sorter with star performance.

2. **The basic three:** Color is the key criterion for sorting laundry loads, and the basic three groups are whites, darks, and mixed. Separate along these color lines, and you have an excellent chance of pulling clothes from the washer representing the same spot on the spectrum as they did when they went in. Cross the lines and all bets are off.

Red, black, and other dark colors can bleed, especially in hot water — so unless you're trying to dye your entire wardrobe pink or gray, sort these into a separate load and use cold water. If something does run, *don't* put the affected garments in the dryer, which will set the color. Rewash them, perhaps with a blast of bleach for whites or nonchlorine bleach for colors.

3. **The not-so-basic 11:** While the basic three categories can take care of singles, couples, and small young families, larger families and active kids can call for advanced sorting calculus that accounts for both volume — how much can fit in the machine at one time — and temperature. Leotards, shorts, and sport tops for gymnastics, cheerleading, and the health club need cold water, but all those plain white T-shirts can go gray if they don't get washed hot. If you're really down in the laundry trenches, your categories may look more like whites with no dark design (hot), light mixed (warm), dark mixed (cold), sheets (hot or warm), towels (hot or warm), white dress shirts and blouses (cold), dark dress shirts and blouses (cold), knits (cold), jeans (warm), sweat clothes (warm or cold), and pajamas (warm).

Here's a place where a little organization can pay off in spades: Treat stains right away. Your chances of saving the garment are higher the sooner you mount your counterattack. Keep a second set of stain-removal products in the master bathroom if the trip to the laundry room tends to delay your treatment efforts. Contain lingerie in mesh bags before washing, nylons in one and bras in another. Close up bra hooks to keep them from catching other clothes. Separate bags for each person make sorting easier when the wash is done. Finally, zip up all the zippers and turn printed T-shirts inside out to protect the design.

Take oversized items such as comforters and bedspreads to a coin laundry with large-capacity machines. Large-sized washables can get cleaner and better rinsed, and won't test the limits of your own machines.

Drying without Crying

Just ask my kids: I can shrink anything. I'm afraid to say that even after two decades, operator error is probably to blame for all the wardrobe downsizing I've done. Shrinking clothes by mistake wastes the money you spent in the store and the time lost in the laundry room, so direct from the school of hard knocks, I present these do's and don'ts for drying without crying:

✔ Remove dryer lint each time to optimize the machine's efficiency and prevent setting your clothes on fire. This, of course, will save you lots of time and trouble.

✔ Match the cycle setting to the load so that the temperature and timing are at least in the right ballpark. The rule of thumb is that the lighter the fabric, the lower the temperature should be. That puts delicates and permanent press at low, jeans and towels on high — get the picture?

✔ *Don't* count on the *automatic* setting to shut the machine off before your clothes have lost a size or two.

✔ Set the dryer's timer with a conservative eye. Most loads are done in 40 minutes or so (less for delicates). Schedule your trip back to the dryer accordingly and plan to pull shrink-sensitive items such as 100 percent cotton garments out while they're still slightly damp and then hang them up to air dry. Finish off the rest with an additional 10 to 15 minutes.

> ✔ *Don't* leave clothes sitting in the dryer after the cycle is done. Cooling in a heap can wrinkle clothes, while hanging or folding them hot will leave them smooth to save you ironing time.

Whether you're trying to outwit a wily dryer or air drying delicates straight from the washer, you need drying systems more advanced than chair backs and doorknobs. Check out Figure 7-4 for a dandy drying idea.

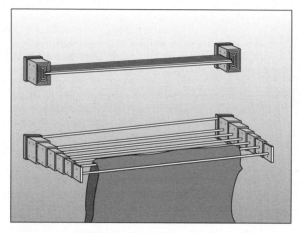

Figure 7-4: A telescoping wire rack for draping small items does a lot of drying in a little bit of space.

The quickest way to get clean laundry back to where it belongs is to sort as you pull washing from the machines. Hanging is generally easier than folding, as anything that comes out damp has a chance to air dry, and you can easily sort by owner as you hang things on a clothes rod or rack or a wall-mounted wire shelf. Whether you're hanging items or folding them into piles, sort by person first; then, depending upon your space and the number of people you're dealing with, you can subsort by garment type — shirts, pants, socks and underwear, and so forth.

 Do you find yourself trying to squeeze a dozen different piles of folded laundry onto the tops of two small machines? Simplify your life with a sorting table with space for all your piles. See Figure 7-3 for a double-duty model with sorting bags below.

Getting It Straight: Ironing

I hate to iron. Maybe it's genetic. My mother couldn't tackle the pile of wrinkly things without our weekly cleaning lady and me by her side. Against my will, I discovered that at least things went faster if you iron right.

Before you even start ironing, equip yourself with a reliable iron, ironing board, and cover. Using the kitchen table instead of a board only makes the job harder and puts you and your clothes at risk. If you're short on space, look for a board that hangs from a door that can be pulled down for use. Occasional ironers can also opt for a mini-board with folding legs that fits in a drawer. Though patterned ironing board covers might be pretty, solids make it easier to see the item you're ironing and get all the wrinkles the first time around.

An iron with automatic shut-off can prevent a safety hazard if you should go to answer the phone or stir the tomato sauce midjob.

Okay, here is your basic, no-frills, quick-and-efficient ironing strategy:

1. **Start with garments that need the lowest heat setting, and then work your way up the dial.** Otherwise, you're sitting around waiting for the iron to cool down between settings, or burning or melting something with your impatience.

2. **Do the fussy parts first — collars, yokes, cuffs, and waistbands.**

3. **Once the small stuff is out of the way, do the sleeves.** Then work from one end of the garment to the other without skipping around.

Never leave a hot iron with the plate flat. After use, pour out any water and stand it on its heel on top of the washer or dryer with the cord well away from the hot side. Don't return the iron to a plastic organizing caddy until it's completely cool, or you'll have a meltdown on your hands.

My favorite ironing tactic is preventive: permanent press. Why buy 100 percent cotton when there are so many great fabrics out there that come out of the dryer ready to wear?

Scheduling Your Laundry Day

Accustomed to doing laundry when you run out of clothes? There is a better way. There are two basic theories about how to schedule your wash: all on one day, or split into two. If you work every day, you may want to leave weekends free for errands, outings, and fun, in which case splitting up the job into one week-night for linens and another for clothes would be best. On the other hand, if you have a young family, you may prefer to get the whole thing out of the way on Saturday or Sunday, when your spouse or a baby-sitter can take the kids or a play date can be arranged. Either way, if you find yourself frequently staring at an empty closet, your schedule needs refining.

Utility or Mudroom

The laundry room often doubles as a mudroom off the back or basement door, where everything from sandy beach towels to crusty boots can congregate. Your utility room may serve as an extra storage spot, or a place to do anything messy. The more hats your laundry room wears, the more you need to organize.

The mess-free mudroom

Though you may not think of the mudroom as wearing a public face, this is a primary point of entry to the house, and family and guests alike may troop through after swimming, picnicking, or playing. Make it nice and easy:

- ✔ Add a closed cabinet for beach towels, and bath towels and supplies if you have a shower and/or bathroom here. See Chapter 4 for more on setting up a beautiful and functional bath area.

- ✔ Use a closed cabinet or shoe rack for sports shoes and organize them by owner.

- ✔ Keep sports clothes neat with designated hanging space, baskets on shelves, or a stand-alone cabinet. Whether it's tae kwon do robes or tennis hats, these things have to go somewhere.

- ✔ Sports equipment can generally be relocated to the garage for easiest access. But if you're short on space there or this is the closest place to grab it as you walk out the door, use an organizing rack to keep equipment neat.

Utility unlimited

Utility means useful, which often translates as storage. If you have more space than you need to get the wash done, consider these additional storage uses for the laundry room:

- ✔ **Extra refrigerator and/or freezer.**

- ✔ **Holiday serving pieces and supplies.** Install shelves, or closed cabinets are better.

- ✔ **Hobby and craft supplies.** If you don't have a dedicated area and usually do your work close by — for instance, if the laundry room is on the first floor and you stage your craft sessions in the kitchen, then store crafts here. Shelving or cabinets are crucial here, and if there are small children in the house it should be high.

- ✔ **Patio cushions.** Though outdoor things generally go in the garage, storing cushions inside keeps them nice and clean for more dignified seating.

- ✔ **Return and repair center.** Pro: Storing your damaged goods in need of fixing or refunds here keeps them out of the way. Con: This room can be way out of mind, and you may never make the trip. Install open shelving that can both organize your return/repair items and make them more obvious.

Cleaning up the laundry room can leave you better dressed and less stressed. Don't get sidelined by stains or worried by wrinkles. Get organized!

Home & Home Repair & Maintenance

Home Improvement All-in-One For Dummies
Roy Barnhart, James Carey, Morris Carey, et al.
978-0-7645-5680-7 · $29.99

Home Improvement For Dummies
Gene Hamilton & Katie Hamilton
978-0-7645-5005-8 · $19.99

Home Maintenance For Dummies, 2nd Edition
James Carey & Morris Carey
978-0-470-43063-7 · $21.99

How to Fix Everything For Dummies
Gary Hedstrom, Peg Hedstrom & Judy Tremore
978-0-7645-7209-8 · $19.99

Kitchen Remodeling For Dummies
Donald R. Prestly
978-0-7645-2553-7 · $19.99 · 8-page color insert

Living the Country Lifestyle All-in-One For Dummies
978-0-470-43061-3 · $29.99

Organizing Do-It-Yourself For Dummies
Sandra Munson
978-0-470-43111-5 · $19.99 · Full Color

Painting Do-It-Yourself For Dummies
Katharine Kaye McMillan & Patricia Hart McMillan
978-0-470-17533-0 · $16.99 · Full Color

Plumbing Do-It-Yourself For Dummies
Donald R. Prestly
978-0-470-17344-2 · $16.99 · Full Color

Green Building & Remodeling For Dummies
Eric Corey Freed
978-0-470-17559-0 · $21.99

Maintenance

Bathroom Remodeling For Dummies
Gene Hamilton & Katie Hamilton
978-0-7645-2552-0 · $19.99 · 8-page color insert

Energy Efficient Homes For Dummies
Rik DeGunther
978-0-470-37602-7 · $21.99